CLASH OF THE MIND AND HEART

PARENTS' PLAYBOOK FOR HELPING YOUTHS SUCCEED

NICHOLAS GABRIEL LIM

Singapore University of Social Sciences, Singapore

NEW JERSEY · LONDON · SINGAPORE · BEIJING · SHANGHAI · HONG KONG · TAIPEI · CHENNAI · TOKYO

Published by

World Scientific Publishing Co. Pte. Ltd.
5 Toh Tuck Link, Singapore 596224
USA office: 27 Warren Street, Suite 401-402, Hackensack, NJ 07601
UK office: 57 Shelton Street, Covent Garden, London WC2H 9HE

British Library Cataloguing-in-Publication Data
A catalogue record for this book is available from the British Library.

CLASH OF THE MIND AND HEART
~~Parents'~~ Playbook for Helping Youths Succeed

Copyright © 2022 by World Scientific Publishing Co. Pte. Ltd.

All rights reserved. This book, or parts thereof, may not be reproduced in any form or by any means, electronic or mechanical, including photocopying, recording or any information storage and retrieval system now known or to be invented, without written permission from the publisher.

For photocopying of material in this volume, please pay a copying fee through the Copyright Clearance Center, Inc., 222 Rosewood Drive, Danvers, MA 01923, USA. In this case permission to photocopy is not required from the publisher.

ISBN 978-981-125-260-0 (hardcover)
ISBN 978-981-125-335-5 (paperback)
ISBN 978-981-125-261-7 (ebook for institutions)
ISBN 978-981-125-262-4 (ebook for individuals)

For any available supplementary material, please visit
https://www.worldscientific.com/worldscibooks/10.1142/12732#t=suppl

Desk Editor: Sandhya Venkatesh

Typeset by Stallion Press
Email: enquiries@stallionpress.com

CLASH OF THE MIND AND HEART
PARENTS' PLAYBOOK FOR HELPING YOUTHS SUCCEED

Foreword

When Nicholas Gabriel Lim invited me to contribute the foreword for this book, which is a resource for understanding youths and helping them succeed, I readily agreed. I have known Nicholas for several years now, seeing his work on youths first when he shared his expertise and experiences at meetings and subsequently as a friend who shared with me his worldview and personal aspirations. In addition to our friendship, there are three reasons why I accepted the invitation.

First, Nicholas has written this book in a clear and concise manner, translating complex issues and some core research findings on youths into simple terms that many will find it relatable and easy to understand. The chapters in the book cover a relatively wide range of issues and evidence relevant to understanding youths, with a useful summary at the end of each chapter to reiterate the key points. Collectively, the chapters will provide a useful and accessible resource for the general public, with little technical jargon, that will enable readers to have a basic framework to think about issues relevant to youth development.

Second, the book has a good mix of principles derived from both the scientific research literature and Nicholas' professional practice and personal experiences. By carefully linking these different knowledge sources, the book provides a balanced and useful analysis of important issues such as recognizing the roles of rationality and emotions and paying attention to approaches that prevent the negatives and promote the positives. The analysis also goes beyond academic understanding to translate the various principles into simple toolkits and other practical recommendations on steps to take, or checklists to consider, when facing complex issues involving youth development and engagement.

Third, by writing this book, Nicholas himself has demonstrated that passion can co-exist with professionalism. His belief in the potential of our youths, zeal in youth engagement and development, and concern for youth well-being is evident in all chapters of the book. Over the past two decades, much has been said in Singapore about engaging youths and the need for people to step up to both speak up and take action. We need to create a climate that encourages such personal initiatives. By translating his passion and professionalism to produce a practical resource for not only parents but anyone interested in youth matters, Nicholas is a good example of younger Singaporeans driven by their passion to step up to contribute to society.

I am confident that this book will be widely read, and more importantly, serve as a springboard or point of departure for many individuals to learn more about youth development and apply the knowledge to their real life situations to make a positive difference.

David Chan
Professor of Psychology
Singapore Management University

Dedicated To

My Mother

My Wife

Paul and Annabelle Long

My youth-clients and their families

About the Author

Nicholas Gabriel Lim is a registered psychologist based in Singapore. He has worked with youth for two decades. He is the co-founder of the Youth Work Association (Singapore) and the author of the widely distributed eBook *Clash of the Mind and Heart: Understanding Adolescents*. He is also a clinical supervisor to young, budding psychologists as well as a youth mentor.

Nicholas spent his career working with the young and their families, in the charity, private and public sectors. Given the depth and breadth of his work with youths, he has been on various government advisory councils in Singapore, like the Media Literacy Council and the National Council for Problem Gambling. Nicholas was recently appointed by the President of Singapore to be an Adviser to the Singapore Youth Court.

While you can call him Nicholas or Gabriel, he is fondly known as Nick or Mr. Nick to his youth-clients. He not only has degrees in Psychology from the University of Queensland, Australia, and the Nanyang Technological University, Singapore, but also various clinical and practice certificates such as for Youth Work Coaching and Supervision, Choice Theory and Reality Therapy, Adventure Therapy, and Therapeutic Behavior Management, to name just a few.

Inspired by some of his work within the juvenile justice system, specifically at the Family Justice Courts, he is currently pursuing his law degree with a focus on family and criminal law. In his free time, Nick enjoys reading good books, swimming, and exercising at the gym. He has three children with his beautiful wife.

With deep knowledge about and extensive experiences with adolescents and their families, Nicholas presents to you some very important insights about adolescents and how they may be engaged, supported, and empowered for success!

For more about Nicholas and his work, you may visit his website: www.nicholasgabriellim.com

Acknowledgments

This book would not have been possible without the encouragement of a special couple, Paul and Annabella Long. Paul and Annabella are advocates for the family in the community. Paul used to be the Executive Director of Family Life Society, a non-profit organization with the mission to empower families. Annabella used to head the Parent Support Group at Saint Gabriel's Secondary School in Singapore.

The inspiration for the content for this book comes from my own family and all the adolescents I have worked with and am still working with. I would not have been the person and practitioner I am today without them. In my family, both my mother, Angela, and my wife, Geraldine, were instrumental and pillars of my adolescence and professional success, respectively. They each kept me laser-focused on my tasks and mission at various stages. As for all the adolescents and the families I have worked with, they challenged me to be better at my craft and deepened my conviction toward doing a good job in my own family and obviously my work with adolescents!

A big thank you! This book is dedicated to you!

Endorsements

Nicholas has written this book in a clear and concise manner, translating complex issues and some core research findings on youths into simple terms that many will find it relatable and easy to understand. The chapters in the book cover a relatively wide range of issues and evidence relevant to understanding youths, with a useful summary at the end of each chapter to reiterate the key points. Collectively, the chapters will provide a useful and accessible resource for the general public, with little technical jargon, that will enable readers to have a basic framework to think about issues relevant to youth development.

David Chan
Professor of Psychology, Singapore Management University

This book is a must-read for all parents, educators, social workers, counsellors and anyone who work with youths or desire for the next generation to have the best chance of success in life. From his years of study of how youths are wired, and direct experience working with youths and parents, the author Nicholas has produced a book that is not only fully backed up by Science, but also filled with stories and tips for immediate application. If you are one of the many who are still seeking answers to parenting or helping a teen, look no further. I encourage you to read this book for yourself, and after that, share this resource with as many as possible.

Jason Wong
Founder, Dads for Life & Yellow Ribbon Project

I first met Nicholas when I co-founded The Young Entrepreneur Mastery (TYEM) academy. He was helping out-of-school youth-clients to develop an entrepreneurial mindset, which I was advocating and teaching!

Years on, we are still in the youth work scene together. His passion for working with youths has not dwindled, and he is able to articulate it with much crisp now. This is clearly reflected in his book. It is evident that neuroscience informs his practice, and he shares it with conviction. There is so much depth to it. Yet, it is not technical. It is readable and relatable. He provides you with a good understanding of why adolescents are the way they are, and why adults are also the way they are, and there is no way both can see, "eye-to-eye". Therein lies the "clash". This is not an impasse. It is an opportunity for personal and relational growth. There is hope!

Therefore, wherever you are in your relationship with your teens, it is never too late to learn how to (re)engage them. Nicholas has something to offer. The best is yet to come! Take Action today!

Elim Chew
Former Youth Ambassador in Singapore
Mentor to many youths and aspiring entrepreneurs/social entrepreneurs
Advisory Board Member, Comeback World, a gaming-dependence support agency

Chairman, I'm KIM Korean BBQ and Goro Goro Steamboat,
One Sushi Group of Restaurants
Chair and Co-chair of several public service, youth and
community groups
Recipient of the Singapore Public Service Medal (PBM) 2011
Founder of 77th Street, a youth fashion and lifestyle retail
Forbes Asia Hero of Philanthropy 2010

Nicholas has brought years of experience working with parents and youths into this book. The insightful perspectives will be refreshing for many out there who are handling and working with our young people today. Keep learning and growing as we empower more young people today!

Joe Chan
Head of Youth Service, REACH Community Services

A wonderful piece of review and contribution in the area of youth work and other specializations. Nicholas has presented a comprehensive literature and content from his years of experiences and a great content for the professionals and many who want to explore working with clients with a specific concern.

Dr. Roland Yeow
Executive Director, Boys' Town

Nicholas sheds light on the inner workings of a youth‚Äôs development, and how we can be a catalyst for their positive development. In a world where growing expectations increasingly weigh heavy on a young person's mental health, this book is an invaluable guide on how we serve as a youth‚Äôs psychological and emotional safe space, all while explaining why that role is key in their journey towards adulthood. Having supported and served alongside youths for more than 16 years, I am confident to say that this book should be a staple for parents and anyone who wants to be a change-maker for the next generation!

Nicholas Lee
Executive Director Resilience Collective
Former Chief Executive Trybe Limited, Managing Agent Singapore Boys' Hostel

This book opened up the door to have better insights into adolescents. Many parents have many issues connecting with and understanding them. This equips us with all the tools we can use so that we can better engage the teenagers. This is a must-read book for every parent. Ultimately, with a better understanding and handling of cases, this will help to reduce family violence and create mutual understanding between parent and the adolescent.

Raymond Chua
Chairman for Dads@CatholicHigh, Catholic High School
Chairman for Parents' Support Group (PROED)
Hwa Chong Institution

Nicholas has a deep understanding of teenagers and their "dance" with the adults around them, which is evident throughout the chapters in his book.

Dr Carol Balhetchet
Clinical Psychologist & Psychotherapist, Dr Carol & Associates
Former Senior Director and Clinical Psychologist of Youth Services, Singapore Children's Society

This is a book I greatly recommend to all parents, educators, youth workers, youth mentors or anyone who works with youths. Nicholas is able to marry both the SCIENCE as well as the heART in connecting and working with youths. And he is able to capture the interest of the reader. I guarantee you will not find it boring. I have personally been very blessed and impacted by this book.

Iris Lin
Deputy Director
Fei Yue Community Services

Nicholas, drawing on his years of experience and practice wisdom, imparts very practical advice and tips for anyone interested in impacting teens and adolescents. While the book seems an easy-read, the principles and strategies it espouses may be challenging, considering that the subject matter focuses on adolescents. That's why it is great that the book provides a useful framework to guide and facilitate progress while applying the concepts. As a fellow practitioner of positive youth development, I wholeheartedly recommend anyone desiring to connect with adolescents to pick up a copy.

Dr John K E Tan
Founding President
Youth Work Association (Singapore)

I have had the privilege of working with Nicholas during my professional work at Family Life Society.

Through my experience working with Nicholas, I have known him to be passionate about engaging youth as well as parents. He is very well-trained and a highly qualified psychologist. I have run numerous parenting workshops conducted by him, and it was always a full house! He is so popular and a very sought-after speaker, especially after he launched his eBook on *Clash of the Mind and Heart: Understanding Adolescents*. He loves to help youth succeed.

Nicholas is also very selfless in sharing his time and resources to help parents overcome challenges they encounter with their adolescent children. He has delivered great value to parents; families have benefitted from it and improved their relationship with their kids. Nicholas is also very generous and would not hesitate to help parents who encounter challenges with their teens after workshops he conducts for parents and teens.

I deeply appreciate his commitments. He is very knowledgeable in youth work. In this book, he shares them generously and provides real ground experiences. He has developed many of his own materials and this is just another good piece he is adding to his repertoire for anyone working with youths. Many of the parents we served at Family Life Society benefitted greatly from Nicholas, Äô trainings and sharing. Parents often appreciate deeply the real help and handles provided by Nicholas. This book consolidates all these and more!

Nicholas is also a loving family man who practices what he preaches. Volunteerism is what is always on his mind when he helps the community. He never expects anything in return. This book bares his continued gifting and the ultimate secrets of understanding and connecting with adolescent children, students, and or clients. I know the clients I previously served have all benefitted from his professional work, I am certain readers of this book will benefit greatly from him here as well.

Paul Long
Former Executive Director
Family LIfe Society

The book by Nicholas is very poignant at this stage because youths are facing tremendous social, psychological and ecological changes, which are likely to have impacts on their families and in their pursuits for meaningful lives. I must state that this a rather comprehensive local piece of youth work which will be most relevant for parents, teachers, youth workers, counsellors and those involved in the care sector. The various chapters of the publication are indeed illustrious and carry psycho-neurological analyses of the mind and body, and other key developmental changes facing youths. It is also interesting that factors contributing to adolescent difficulties are discussed well and with good case presentations. Nicholas, with his grassroots experiences, is able to give insights as to how one can work effectively with youths and those who are vulnerable. One should not miss this interesting local perspective on youths and in the process acquire some skills to engage them to be valued human beings.

Emeritus Professor S Vasoo
Department of Social Work
National University of Singapore

Parenthood is hard work. Despite all the education that we have gone through, nothing prepares a parent for parenthood. And parenting an adolescent? I know first-hand how difficult that can be, and I find myself rolling with the punches. Most times, I think I just end up proverbially punched. So thank you Nicholas, for this invaluable book, which I will take time to digest, so that I can be a better parent for my kids (and my sanity).

I have had the privilege of working alongside Nicholas in his capacity as a Psychologist in the Family Justice Courts over a variety of difficult cases, and he has been stellar in his professionalism and ability to capture the essence of any dispute. Nicholas has a gentleness that encourages tough teens and adults to talk, coupled with nerves of steel when faced with difficult, angry persons.

With simplicity and honesty, this book tackles the difficult areas of parental reactions that exacerbate difficult adolescent behaviour. His real-life examples strike a familiar chord with most parents, and his solutions are practical and non-judgemental. I appreciate too, the summaries at the end of each chapter to ensure the take-aways for busy parents. This book reminds me that I am part of a community of parents, all feeling the exact same emotions and the same helplessness. And then somehow, we don't seem so alone anymore.

"Start children off on the way they should go: when they grow old, they will not depart from it." Proverbs 22:6. May we all learn something from Nicholas' book to start our children off on the way that they should go.

Lim Choi Ming
Family Justice Courts, Singapore

Kudos to Nicholas for collating some of the neuro-scientific evidences and theories that may help us guide youths through the challenging years of growing up. Reading this book makes us realise how much work a parent or formator has to do — may we be the first to improve! With the help of Nicholas' experience and research we can try to make inroads into the psyche of young people, to discover, understand, enjoy and even admire what goes on in that developing mind. His balanced approach combines the best of a prudential use of freedom with the close accompaniment and guidance that parents should give. With this book, we learn how to capitalise on the positive aspects of the limbic system and create the ambience needed for the pre-frontal cortex to develop its far-reaching potential.

Dr Alvin Wong, MD
The Bigger Picture program
Ravenahl Study Centre

Each teen develops differently, therefore, there are no hard and fast rules to be applied as each teen is a unique individual with different culture, family background and support. In trying to understand the challenges faced by adolescents and how parents can be guided to find out more, understanding the developmental stages of the youths' brains shared in this book are good reference points for a start.

Understanding that a youth's action is basically controlled by the growth of his brain in stages can help parents to have a deeper insight into their teenager's apparently discordant behaviour. Nicholas sliced the brain apart to explain how different parts of it affect the teenagers' development. He further explains how the gulf between parents and adolescents can be bridged by understanding that adolescents are keen to have fun and excitement, as opposed to doing mundane things like finishing the homework first before playing games. Teenagers who feel supported and understood can then confide in their parents when they encounter issues. I hope that readers will find some solutions to the problems that they face when dealing with adolescents from this useful guide.

Ellen Lee, JP, PBM
President, Silver Ribbon (Singapore)

Contents

Foreword v

About the Author ix

Acknowledgments xi

Endorsements xiii

Chapter 1   Introduction   1

Chapter 2   Relationship First   9

Chapter 3   Youth Brain — Part 1   21

Chapter 4   Youth Brain — Part 2   41

Chapter 5   It Takes a Village   65

Chapter 6   Intentional Engagement   77

Chapter 7   Mind of Dopamine   91

Chapter 8   Five Cognitive Controls   99

Chapter 9   Developing High-Level Thinking   125

Chapter 10 The Power of Presence   145

Chapter 11 Learning What Does Not Work   163

Chapter 12 Things That Work   183

Chapter 13 Five Things to Avoid   207

Chapter 14 The Challenges and Beyond   223

Chapter 15 Conclusion   257

Real-Life Stories   265
Supplementary Resources For You   279

Chapter 1

Introduction

Welcome! I am excited that you have this book in your hand! This book is filled with lots of heartache, tears, laughter, pride, and hope. It is a book that captures almost twenty years of youth work I have been in and still counting, and the fundamentals you need to know about working with youth, where learning points are derived from **not only my personal experiences but also my professional training.**

The heartache is there because some youth may never respond to you positively, or in the way you hope they will; even if they do respond to you positively, they may make decisions or act in ways that may cause your heart to break. It will hurt because much time and effort has been put into working with them, and it seems like everything has gone down the drain because of a bad move or decision on their part.

There are tears and laughter as well because hanging out with them makes you connect with their humanity. The term "hanging out" is commonly understood as being physically present with the youth wherever they like to go or be at, regardless of whether there was anything to do, meaningfully or otherwise.

When you hang out with youth, there are so many things they talk about. They may talk about the latest online games they are playing; they may talk about their family; they may talk about their vices; they may talk about their fears and aspirations; they may even poke fun at their friends, or sometimes just be a blatherskite. It is through times spent with them like this that you hear about their struggles, pain, or confusion, and even their hopes, dreams, and goals. You cannot help sometimes but cry with them and even laugh with them because you can literally see the tension or hurt they are experiencing, say, with their parents, or see the pain they are in because of a betrayal by a close friend, or even the excitement of achieving better results because of the hard work they put into their studies, or how happy they are when they get to go on a holiday with their family.

Also, when youth invite you to their graduation, or provide some testament to your efforts in helping them achieve their goals, or for being instrumental in their success, you will inevitably feel proud and also feel a sense of fulfillment. Success with them normally happens when the youth respond positively not only to you but also to anyone who is in their life, helping, supporting, encouraging, and motivating them along. Of course, responding to you positively is insufficient; they would have to put in the hard work as well. It brings hope not only to them when they see themselves succeed but to us as well. It means they know they can overcome and excel, and the adults too know that their efforts are not wasted, and there is hope that the youth may come out alright, better still rise above all odds!

Therefore, to celebrate all that, and to continue to give hope to all parents and possibly youth work practitioners who might pick up this book as well, I have put together this sequel to my digital book *The Clash of the Mind and Heart.* Those interested may scan the QR code at the end of this book to receive the digital for free. I have been educating parents and helping them understand youth for almost a decade now with the digital book. In this book, we dive deeper into all the sciences and concepts introduced.

There is obviously a lot of information out there about understanding youth. I often ask myself if what I have to offer makes any difference, and if it is even adding value to the lives of families, schools, and communities.

The usual feedback I get is about the usefulness and effectiveness of *brain theory*, which is often not understood clearly when trying to successfully engage youth. It is evidence based and well researched. Understanding it not only helps parents appreciate youth behavior better but it also helps the adults manage personal expectations and self-regulate their emotions.

POSITIVE YOUTH DEVELOPMENT

At the same time, it is about *positive youth development.* When engaging youth, it is also about engaging the various systems that the youth are in. It is an intentional pro-social approach in engaging youth along with their systems of support like friends or social networks, family, school, community, and government so that the youth are empowered to reach their full potential.

What is the goal in positive youth development? It is to leverage the strengths of the youth to achieve positive outcomes, at the same time providing opportunities, fostering positive relationships, and equipping the support systems needed to enhance the young person's leadership strengths. Leadership is understood here broadly as leading one's life in a positive manner, making and creating positive impacts along the way.

All this starts with parents; while every parent wants to play a part in their children's lives, there may be limitations for families to be involved in the most desired manner. Limitations could be a lack of time, inadequate knowledge or skills, and even life circumstances. Therefore, this book proposes a framework adapted from Search Institute's Developmental Relationship Framework on *what* to work on when engaging youth for parents, and *how* to do so using strategies guided by neuroscience. It has been tried and tested, and responses have been mostly positive, barring any developmental dysfunctions and special needs the young person might have congenitally or developed along the way.

DEVELOPMENTAL RELATIONSHIPS

Search Institute is a non-profit organization that studies and works to strengthen youth success in schools, youth programs, families, and communities. The Institute was a pioneer in using social science to understand the lives, beliefs, and values of young people. Over the years, they have conducted studies and projects with more than 5 million children and adolescents, published more than 30 books, nearly 150 journal articles and chapters, and introduced new frameworks, tools, and approaches, such as developmental relationships that build on insights gleaned from their research-based foundational framework in positive youth development called Developmental Assets®. We shall discuss more about the proposed framework in the next chapter. It will help us focus on not only what to do to enhance the relationship we have with our teens but it should also inform us about *why* it is so important to know what to do and how to do it. At the heart of everything we are doing or trying to do, is for our relationship with the youth, which matters greatly to us.

NEUROSCIENCE

When it comes to the *how*, neuroscience provides us with the answers. Research informs us that there is a difference in the cognitive and emotional development of youth compared to adults. I discussed this in my digital book to some extent to help parents grasp this at the most fundamental level. In this book, we will dive very deep into it. These two types of development — cognitive and emotional — are not parallel in the physical maturation rates within the brain. Experts compared magnetic resonance images of teenagers and adults and showed how cognitive development does not happen at the same time as emotional development in adolescents.

When the images of adults' brains were taken under the condition of fear, the limbic area of the brain, emotion center, and the prefrontal cortex, judgment and reasoning center, were equally enhanced. Meanwhile, in the adolescents' brains, the same images displayed the limbic area enhanced, with the prefrontal cortex showing no activity. This is evidence for early development of emotions.

This is the reason why we think that the "mind and heart" of the adolescents are constantly "clashing" during their teenage years — parents want them to study hard, for example, but they would rather hang out with their friends, sometimes even at the expense of their sleep or examination results. Why? Their "logic" seems illogical many times.

The imbalance between the prefrontal and limbic responses is real and it is biological. The Limbic System is fully developed during puberty, at about 10–15 years of age. The prefrontal cortex, however, begins to develop during puberty and becomes fully mature only around the age of 20–25 years. **This is 10 years apart!** One obvious reason for this is that the brain matures from the back to the front.

We are going to discuss this more extensively later in Chapter 3. So, I will hold my horses for now. The goal of discussing this neuroscience information is to help parents understand and appreciate their teenagers at the developmental stage they are in, and to learn to adopt strategies that can target this very aspect. The more proficiently we execute the strategies, the better we are able to correct, modify, and even influence the thinking and behaviors of our youth, especially those aspects that are undesirable. I have proposed some strategies, but feel free to use those that you know as well and those that you are comfortable using instead.

Essentially, you want to understand and know if the strategy you are going to use is a limbic strategy or a prefrontal strategy, and if you are aware of when to use which strategy given the presenting reactions or behaviors from your teenager — are you stimulating the prefrontal or the limbic part of the brain? If you use a prefrontal strategy when your child is highly negative emotionally, your teen may not be ready to listen or engage with you, let alone do what you instruct. A rule of thumb is that if your teenager is negatively "limbic" or emotional, you do not want to use prefrontal strategies or any negative emotions to engage the child; more on this later.

RECOMMENDATIONS

The content in this book could be read linearly or topically, and parents may selectively choose what content is most relevant, practical, or even doable. Minimally, I recommend understanding the youth brain and the need for deep positive relationship with your teen. While one strategy or approach may work with a particular child or family, it may not necessarily work with another, simply because every child is unique.

Parents should take note that I may use the words "youth," "adolescents," "child," "children," "students," "teens," "teenagers," "young persons," and all its likes interchangeably. They are expected to mean the same thing. The target population we are discussing here is persons between the age range of 10 and 25 years, inclusive of a variance of 5 years. The variance is to account for the different rates of development each person goes through for a variety of reasons, like nutrition, environment, culture, medication, and even developmental dysfunctions, to name just a few.

In this book, I also hope to capture the motivation behind the work I have done for so many years with youth and parents, and to expand substantially the material in my digital book. You can expect to see more researched information and applications of the theories relating to the brain, with the added frameworks guiding your application and intervention to have a stronger relationship with your child. I wish every parent and family success in relationship building and engagement with your youth.

Chapter 2

Relationship First

When it comes to the development of young people, relationships are very important. I cannot stress this enough. It is no longer a cliché! Everyone I know in education and in the youth work profession agrees, preaches, and advocates that relationships are vital for young people's learning, growth, and thriving. Unfortunately, our societies and communities today still continue to underinvest in and even undermine developmental relationships. This is particularly so when it comes to young people from marginalized communities who most need and want them.

The idea that relationships are key not only has a strong research backing, it is a daily necessity. It is found that high-quality relationships are essential for a young person's growth, learning, and thriving — more so for those young people who face serious challenges in their lives and in the world around them. Therefore, for our learning purposes, we will be looking into Search Institute's framework on Developmental Relationships[1] to guide us on *what*

---

[1] The Developmental Relationships Framework, Search Institute, accessed 20 June 2020, https://www.search-institute.org/developmental-relationships/developmental-relationships-framework.

to work on when we talk about engaging youth. To introduce the framework, I will share a little bit about myself.

When I was younger, I had a distant relationship with my father. He worked hard and supported the family. He was seldom around. At the same time, I feared my father a lot. I was caned and disciplined by him strictly. He was usually calm, composed, measured, deliberate, and non-communicative while disciplining me. He was either informed of my misbehavior or found my behavior intolerable by his standards.

As a result, I kept to myself a lot and focused on the things I liked to do — mostly play when I was younger. This affected my academic performance significantly and I found myself eligible for secondary schools that not many would like to be associated with. I did badly for my Primary School Leaving Examination (PSLE).

This devastated my mother, as she had worked hard and endured much to provide the best for me. I did not come from a very privileged family. I felt that I had disappointed her, and I was ashamed of myself. There was no one else to blame but myself.

By today's standard, I was highly at risk of harming myself in many ways. Home was a fearful place to return to. I was resentful and blamed myself a lot. I questioned my self-worth and abilities constantly. I was quiet and quite a passive-aggressive kind of person.

Unlike those who might feel better expressing their anger and other strong emotions outwardly, like fighting, I had the tendency to implode by way of isolating myself socially. I had poor social skills and interaction with people and socializing was a problem. I often felt out of place or like an outcast; I did not feel like I belonged. Outwardly, no one guessed that I was deeply troubled, let alone thought I needed help.

Throughout the entire time, there was one person who always believed in me and encouraged me along — my mother! Through my academic and relationship failures, I always had her quiet and unwavering support at the back. She was always there to listen and encourage me. And, I felt that without it, I would not have overcome the numerous challenges in my life — she believed in me — and I would have perished without even a single soul knowing of my existence.

I was obviously motivated to do a lot of things, but never motivated to study. I was motivated in my extracurricular activities in school, of which I had numerous; I was motivated in church activities, which I was heavily committed in; but, I was the least motivated in my studies. I was motivated in these areas because I was highly empowered by my parents. I learnt later in life that my father was distant from me because he subscribed to the idea that boys should be left to navigate the world themselves and stretched for growth. Thankfully, this complimented my mother's approach of being close and warm, being my advocate and voice even when my decisions or choices may not be that sound, like focusing less on my studies. I think this sentence may need a punctuation somewhere. It is a mouthful.

Nonetheless, being my avid supporters throughout those challenging years in secondary school, my parents in their own way helped me learn from my mistakes and setbacks, and I graduated not only at the top of my school cohort academically, during my Cambridge "O" Level Examinations, but I also received the colors or merit awards for having accomplished significant success in all my extracurricular activities — like being the head prefect of the school, the overall in command of the National Cadet Corp (Land) of my school unit, and being the Unit Drill Instructor. The NCC (Land) was the army equivalent for students in schools, the only difference being that it was not conscripted. Students voluntarily underwent moderate army training and earned their stripes through their secondary school education. It was a uniformed group where students learnt jungle craft, weapon handling, and even foot drills. My mother always expected me to do my best; I was at my best and I lived up to my potential. From then, I continued to take on different leadership roles in my life and created impact along the way at various levels in society.

According to Search Institute, it can be said that the *trustworthy* and *purposeful* relationship with my parents helped me thrive. Obviously, while growing up, I never could have seen, known, or felt that my parents were building such a relationship with me. On reflection, it was my mother's quiet and unwavering support, her willingness to always listen to me, and her generosity of heart to constantly encourage me that built in me a trust for her. As a result of all that, she was the person I would trust with what was in my heart while growing up. At the same time, my father's purposeful distancing from me, because he himself was brought up in a similar manner, allowed me to navigate the world by myself and to stretch myself for growth, even if it meant falling and making mistakes.

This kind of relationship is called *developmental* relationship, because it helped me discover who I am, developed my ability to shape my life, and assisted me in learning how to engage with and contribute to the world. I believed I failed my PSLE because I had too much freedom to do whatever I wanted. I recall my father quarreling with my mother to avail such freedom for me. My mother was obviously trying to instill some discipline and responsibility in me, but I chose to play more. However, it was the same freedom that made me choose to make a comeback and focus on climbing my way back up. I was laser focused each step of the way with the usual quiet and unwavering support from my mother. I was not only focused in my studies but I also contributed significantly to my uniformed and church groups. I grew to know what I was capable of doing, and how much I want and can push myself. I had tasted failure and success, and I had the freedom to choose competently and confidently.

It is this same *developmental* relationship that is the *what* that we are going to focus and work on. Search Institute has developed a framework, which I have adapted based on my experience and learning, to guide your efforts in building that *developmental* relationship with your teens.

My parents each had their way of engaging me, and in so doing, helped me become the best version of myself. Search Institute categorized some, if not most, of the actions my parents did with me into a dynamic mix of five elements called the Developmental Relationship Framework. For completeness, Search Institute stipulated only 20 actions, and the framework below is expressed from the perspective of a young person.

Developmental Relationship Framework

Elements	Actions	Definition
Share Power	Respect me	Take me seriously and treat me fairly
	Include me	Involve me in decisions that affect me
	Collaborate	Work with me to solve problems and reach goals
	Let me lead	Create opportunities for me to take action and lead
Express Care	Be dependable	Be someone I can trust
	Listen to me	Pay attention when we are together
	Believe in me	Make me feel known and valued
	Be warm	Show me you enjoy being with me
	Encourage me	Praise me for my efforts and achievements
Expand Possibilities	Inspire me	Inspire me to see possibilities for my future
	Broaden my horizons	Expose me to new ideas, experiences, and places
	Connect me	Introduce me to more people who can help me grow
Challenge Growth	Expect my best	Expect me to live up to my potential
	Stretch me	Push me to go further
	Hold me accountable	Insist I take responsibility for my actions
	Reflect on my failures	Help me learn from mistakes and setbacks

(Continued)

Elements	Actions	Definition
Provide Support	Navigate with me	Guide me through hard situations and systems
	Empower me	Build my confidence to take charge of my life
	Be my advocate	Defend me when I need it
	Set boundaries for me	Put in place limits to keep me on track

According to Search Institute, developmental relationships can also be experienced in a wide range of relationships with different people at home, at school, and in the community. It is said that young people are most likely to do well when they have at least one well-rounded, strong, and sustained relationship in their lives, as well as a broader web of many positive relationships across the places where they spend time and the people with whom they interact.

Some parents at this point may be worried about who their child is building the relationship with and what is happening in the relationship. Rightfully so. All good and responsible parents would be. This is where I like to highlight *developmental* relationships. These are not just any relationships. There are relationships where your child develops confidence, responsibility, respect, etc., from that relationship he or she is in. For example, I obviously learnt trust and patience from my mother. I learnt intentionality from my father. I learnt discipline from my uniformed group leaders and instructors — I learnt to polish my boots, starched my uniform, be on time for parades, etc. I learnt respect and value relationships from my church leaders and pastors. And, I did not learn all these overnight. It was learnt over years of spending time with them, having gone through the ups and downs in life with them, doing projects with them, going to camps, trainings, and classes with them, etc.

I share another example with you. While I was doing research for this book, I read about a person named Josh Shipp.[2] His story is inspiring. Josh was once an abused and raped kid, fostered in homes. He acted out many times, broke the law, and kept to himself a lot because he could not trust anyone. When he was 14 years of age, he met Rodney, his foster father, and that was when his life started to turn around.

Despite Josh's best effort to alienate himself, Rodney just refused to give up on him. Josh testified about how Rodney was that one caring adult who loved him unconditionally and helped him see what he could not — that he was not a problem, but an opportunity. Josh could have become what statistics predicted: dead or in jail. Josh is still alive today; an award-winning speaker and author, a youth advocate, a global youth empowerment expert, and a living proof of the power of being in a developmental relationship with a loving adult. As Josh puts it, the difference between being a statistics and a success story is you! Yes, you parents! Put it in another way,

---

[2] Every Kid is One Caring Adult Away From Being a Success Story, Josh Shipp, accessed 20 June 2020, https://joshshipp.com/.

you want to be that person in a developmental relationship with the youth! Your child.

Like me, Josh had someone like Rodney who showed him that he mattered. Rodney showed his unconditional love despite everything Josh did to push Rodney away. Josh was treated with respect, yet held accountable for his actions. This is developmental relationship in action! When Josh broke the law, he was left to take responsibility for his actions in lock up. Rodney deliberately left Josh in the station overnight. It was only later that Rodney bailed him out and inspired him to recognize the possibilities of his future. Josh felt empowered and confident to take charge of his own life and future thereafter!

At the heart of this book, it is the developmental relationship between parent and youth that we are focusing on and value; it is the developmental relationship between any caring adult and youth. Youth do best when they experience strong, positive relationships in all parts of their lives. And, there is a great deal of research from numerous scholars in many different settings offering evidence that supports this claim.

Research to date has shown that young people who experience strong developmental relationships across different parts of their lives are more likely to show signs of positive development in many areas. Search Institute offers the following findings:

- increased academic motivation;
- increased social–emotional growth and learning;
- increased sense of personal responsibility;
- reduced engagement in a variety of high-risk behaviors.

This is *what* we are aiming to achieve at the end of the day with you parents — strong developmental relationships with your teens. In all the materials we are presenting and discussing, it is meant to help you, parents, achieve strong bonds and relationships with your child. "For what?" you may ask or wonder. This is so that your child may do well academically, have a heightened sense of personal responsibility, show social–emotional growth and development, and not engage in high-risk behaviors.

To assist you along, when we start to discuss strategies that you can use to engage your teens, at the beginning of that chapter, I will provide you a "VOICE Targeting Checklist," like the one shown below, to give you an idea of what you are targeting when you use the strategies discussed in this book.

Essentially, VOICE is the adapted *five elements* from the Developmental Relationship Framework (DRF). It is deliberately reframed into VOICE to reflect back to us, to you parents, that it is really about letting your child's voice be heard. Every child has a voice that wants to be heard. And, I sincerely believe that as parents we do want to hear them and let their voice be heard. However, in most instances, their voices are always drowned by the adults' protectiveness, concerns, worries, fears, and even insecurities. Do not get me wrong; it is not that we should not be protective or concerned about our child's well-being and interests. On the contrary, we should! And, we want to do it in a manner where *the child* feels supported, empowered, confident, and secure, and not otherwise. The framework reflects the voice of the young person because it endeavors to ensure the often drowned voice of the child is heard and understood.

DRF
Targeting Checklist

Developmental Relationship Elements	Check
V VOICE	✓
O SHOW	✓
I INSPIRE	✓
C CHALLENGE	✓
E ENCOURAGE	✓

To ensure that this is crystal clear, let me express it in first-person statements:

"Treat me with respect and give me a say."

V Literally, the teen is asking for his or her **V**OICE to be heard. In doing so, the teen feels respected and understood. The power is felt and shared.

"Show me that I matter to you."

O   Literally, the teen is asking parents to SH**O**W or to express care. In doing so, the teen feels he or she matters! The teen feels valued and important.

"**Inspire** me to go beyond my world and myself."

I   **I**NSPIRE your teens to go beyond their world and expand possibilities, by connecting them with people and places that broaden their horizon. Truly, the teen is asking to be connected, and not online!

"**Challenge** me to keep getting better."

C   The teen is asking parents to push them constantly, so that they can improve and grow. The **C**HALLENGE is by choice, and not by imposition.

"**Encourage** me to complete tasks and achieve goals."

E   The teen is asking parents to **E**NCOURAGE them to take charge and achieve. The key is to provide the support and *not do the tasks* for him or her.

SUMMARY

1. Young people do well when they have at least one well-rounded, strong, and sustained relationship in their lives.
2. Young people do well with a broader web of positive relationships across the places where they spend time and the people with whom they interact.

Chapter 3
Youth Brain — Part 1

I highlighted earlier that experts compared magnetic resonance images of teenagers and adults and showed how cognitive development does not happen at the same time as emotional development in adolescents. The cognitive development and emotional development do not occur in parallel in the physical maturation rates, specifically in the brain.

When the images of adults' brain were taken under the condition of fear, the limbic area of the brain, emotion center, and the prefrontal cortex, judgment and reasoning center, were equally enhanced. Meanwhile, in the adolescents' brain, the same images displayed the limbic area enhanced, with the prefrontal cortex showing no activity. This suggests early development of emotions.

As a result, there is what I call the "clash of the mind and heart" phenomenon during the adolescence period.

The "clash" is a natural part of our growing up, and it is very challenging to go through it, especially for parents. You can imagine that both the limbic and the prefrontal cortex areas of the brain are equally enhanced on the MRI scanners for the parents, when they see their teenager jumping off a ledge almost two stories high, as part of a parkour maneuverer. However, this was something that the youth gladly take on for fun and maybe even to challenge himself or herself for more difficult obstacles subsequently.

Despite discouraging the child umpteen times to take on less risky sports or activities, among many other strategies used and tried, both parents grow more anxious and fearful with each passing day. Here comes the ultimate, the more parents inform the child of all the possible consequences, with all available information, the pros and cons, the less likely the child would move an inch. It seems like a losing battle right from the outset. This is the "clash" we are talking about. And, to make a claim that this is a natural part of growing up might be unsettling for some parents. It seems like every effort made is going to be futile.

Let me put it out there now, it is not futile at all. In fact, it is only the beginning. For now, know for a fact that there is nothing personal when a "clash" happens. It usually requires the parents to know that different parts of the youth brain are receiving and learning the information. This is not so for the youth. Adults are in a better position to re-strategise. It has to be a strategy that is typically not used by an adult. Yes, you read that correctly! "Typically Not Used By An Adult." Otherwise, learning and reception of the message from the adult would not be received effectively.

We will go deeper into this in the next chapter, but for now, the key is to heighten our appreciation of how our brain learns, which will set the stage for understanding the "clash" and how to help the brain learn more specifically, despite the ongoing clashes. In actual fact, the ongoing clash is going to be for a significant period of time; similarly, more about this in the next chapter.

For now, we want to understand how the human brain learns in a broader sense. We learn from Eric Jensen,[1] author of *Teaching with the Brain in Mind*, and an educator, about the three key features relevant to structure and development of the brain.

1. *Adaptability*: The brain changes constantly. This relates to the nature of the brain. It is working, changing, and either declining or improving in performance, depending on the many related reasons.
2. *Integration*: The brain operates with a high level of structural cooperation and competition, on even seemingly simple processes, like learning to read.
3. *Sophistication*: The brain structure is dynamic and versatile, but unlike many things on earth, it is sophisticated and evokes curiosity and wonder.

By focusing on these three aspects, you can see that a set of behaviors which are carefully designed or planned to address the adolescents can be effective and bring about the desired results. In fact, the negative thoughts in our minds and the incorrect interpretation of a youth's behavior misguide us about them. It clogs our mind from appreciating them and encouraging them toward finer behavior which is eventually going to be a part of their thoughts because of adults' positive expectations.

---

[1] Jensen, E. (1998). *Teaching with the Brain in Mind*. Alexandria, VA: Association for Supervision and Curriculum Development.

I recall when I worked with adolescents in schools, we specifically planned a set of behaviors called "catching the good." This was designed to address the youth and counter the stereotype that everything they did amounts to something that was wrong, or that they were up to no good. These can be the negative thoughts in the minds of some adults in schools and in their lives, to the extent that the adults actually believe that their students only know how to misbehave. Like, for the behavior of the student walking to the front of the classroom during lesson time, the adult may think that the child is disrupting the lesson, and punishes the child, when in actual fact, the child actually could not see very well from the back of the classroom, and has already obtained permission to move to the front of the classroom. It was almost inconceivable that the child was capable of asking permission to move to a place in the classroom to learn better.

In adopting the "catching the good" behaviors, we actually *adapt* our responses by pausing for a split second to consider a good reason why a student would want to walk during lesson time to the front of the classroom. Failing to come up with good reasons, we *integrate* our responses with the circumstance, and ask a very logical and sensible question — "What is the reason for standing up to walk?" With much *sophistication* in the brain, the student would begin to wonder — "How come I am not 'called out' for doing something wrong or bad inaccurately? Instead, there is someone interested to know why I am walking in class during lesson time." This is usually refreshing for teens, because they tend to want to be "caught doing good" more, and this gives them the opportunity to say I got permission from the school to sit in front due to my poor eyesight. This would show their ability to act responsibly and deserving of compliments. And finally, to take the behavior straight through, we articulate the praise for the good behaviors and genuinely affirm the child's efforts toward acting responsibly. And, such "catching the good" behavior is something we want to learn to constantly do with youth. Why do we need to do so?

THE BRAIN DEVELOPMENT OF ADOLESCENTS

You see, children's brains grow at an amazing speed and by the time they hit the age of six, their brain is almost 95 percent of an adult brain size. So, what sort of development happens in adolescents? The fact is that it is the remodeling of the human brain that happens intensively during adolescence and continues in the Mid-twenties or even late twenties.

Remodeling is a lot about sorting out, grooming, reshaping, developing, and doing much more. This remodeling is not the same between teenagers themselves, though it starts almost at the same age and in the same way. The difference happens because of the different timing of puberty. So, early puberty means early onset of brain remodeling or adolescent brain development.

WHAT HELPS ADOLESCENT BRAIN DEVELOPMENT

Talking and talking and talking — this is what helps the adolescents. Adults who talk little to children leave them confused, wandering, uncertain, etc. Talking helps children grow up mentally. An environment which is safe and warm with a lot of understanding and support is essential for brain development. Youth look forward to the adults as support to find encouragement; they respond to rewards and not punishments. Clear and consistent boundaries do not offend them; they want their growing ability and capacity to be respected. When they make decisions independently, it is respected.

The growing brain starts connecting practically. Hence, they learn fast and do not actually have to depend on their adults. They seek opportunities to develop their skills, talents, and actions; they want these new developments to be valued. While the brain develops, it produces plenty of new connections which are deleted from the brain if not used. So, adults need to encourage the youth generously to save the new connections by putting them into practice.

This is the time when good habits grow; developing positive habits needs to stay. In other words, the connections need to be wired together. While a teenager is stepping ahead into adulthood, positive habits and thinking can be wired and saved. This is the right time. In fact, it takes a lot of struggle and hard work to rewire adults.

THE BRAIN'S ABILITY TO CHANGE AND ADAPT

The startling facts that have newly emerged from several studies of the brain include the brain's ability to adapt beyond our expectations. Actually, certain activities and motor skills have an everlasting influence on our brain.

Some of the most interesting recent research on the brain's adaptability shows how activities can influence the actual mass and organization of the brain. For example, playing a musical instrument consistently over time can literally remap the brain's "real estate."

Two neuroscientists, one of whom was Arnold Scheibel from the University of California, Los Angeles, conducted an autopsy on a renowned violinist and found that the area of the brain responsible for hearing reception (layer four, auditory cortex) was twice as thick as normal.[2] The other neuroscientist, Michael Kilgard from the University of Texas, Dallas, found that areas of the auditory cortex increased in size with specific auditory training over time.[3] It is as if the brain said, "We need more space for what you are doing. We will just use this nearby spot."

Jensen highlighted in his book a study which found that the cerebellum, the brain structure that contains almost half of the brain's neurons and that is also involved in keeping beat and rhythm, was five percent larger in musicians than in the general population.[4,5] He also mentioned that these studies and others provide evidence that "many years of specific fine-motor exercise prompt brain reorganization and nerve growth."

---

[2] Diamond, M. C., & Hopson, J. (1998). *Magic Trees of the Mind: How To Nurture Your Child's Intelligence, Creativity, and Healthy Emotions from Birth Through Adolescence.* New York: Plume.

[3] Kilgard, M. P., & Merzenich, M. M. (1998). Plasticity of temporal information processing in the primary auditory cortex. *Nature Neuroscience, 1*(8), 727–731.

[4] Gaser, C., & Schlaug, G. (2003). Brain structures differ between musicians and non-musicians. *Journal of Neuroscience, 23*(27), 9240–9245.

[5] Hutchinson, S., Lee, L. H. L., Gaab, N., & Schlaug, G. (2003). Cerebellar volume of musicians. *Cerebral Cortex, 13*(9), 943–949.

It is truly amazing to know that the brain is actually always purposeful. No mysterious power drives it. In fact, it is real-life positive and negative activities that influence our brains.

The brain is the center of multiple systems and the command center, where the governing power is life experiences and the complex processes of varying intensity and precision within it.

Our constantly changing brain shifts our moods, our thinking, and our actions through countless chemical and electrical changes. The state of mind shifts with each of these changes.

The key point here that is central to our topic is that the human brain can change and it actually changes, and the influential factor for change is our life. This understanding is in a sense very broad. I am mindful of that.

To narrow it down, we can say daily habits, activities, reactions, new experiments, the influence of others, shocks, accidents, rewards, pleasures, gains, losses, etc., contribute to human brain change.

Moreover, the human mind does not change because of the influence of things only, but human beings have the **capacity** and the **choice** to change their own brains or influence the brains of others and change it.

This is the reason why adopting a strategy like "catching the good" behaviors is strongly encouraged when working with and engaging youth. They remodel the adult by seeing the good not only in themselves but also in others. They absorb and retain the learning that they had a good experience with and self-select to use the learning for personal benefit. The more they self-select by choice, especially within a supportive environment, the more they retain that learning. Using brain language, neuropathways specific to that learning are formed and serve to help the youth use it purposefully and successfully for their own interest. If the application of this learning impacts the people around them, it will not only influence the brains of others around them but it can also help them transcend beyond their initial learning and apply it in highly integrative and adaptive ways. This is the power of our brains.

BRAIN'S AMAZING ABILITY TO CONNECT

Understanding the intricacy of how the brain develops and grows in the time of adolescence requires that we understand how the human brain is structured.

The brain's various parts and its nerve cells are nearly 1 million miles of nerve fibers. The human brain has the largest area of the uncommitted cortex (with no specific function identified so far) of any species on earth. This gives humans extraordinary flexibility for learning. Scientists divide brain areas into lobes (see Figure 1).

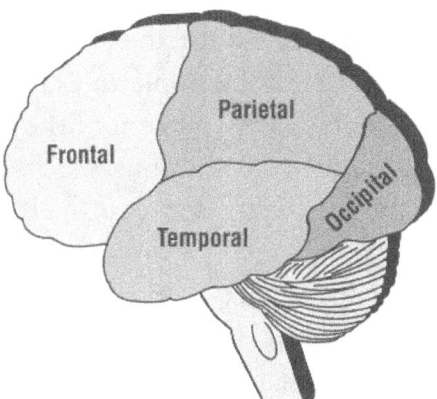

Figure 1: Main areas of the human brain.

The *occipital lobe* is in the middle-back area of the brain, and it is primarily responsible for vision. The *temporal lobes* are located above and around the ears on the left and right sides of the brain. These areas are primarily responsible for hearing, memory, and language. Connect visual areas to language areas, and you can "see" what you hear and say. That's part of the essence of reading: high visual–auditory connectivity.

The *frontal lobe* is the area around your forehead. It is involved with purposeful activities like judgment, creativity, problem-solving, and planning. It also holds short-term memory so you can juggle two or more thoughts at once.

The *parietal lobe* is at the top and back areas of your head. Its duties include processing higher sensory and language functions. It also has a cool tie-in with the Sci-Fi Channel in that it is highly active in subjects who claim to have seen hallucinations or UFOs or have had "near-death" experiences.

The territory in the middle of the brain includes the hippocampus, thalamus, hypothalamus, cingulate, basal ganglia, fornix, striatum, and amygdala (see Figure 2).

You could call this area both the chemistry lab and the drama department of the brain. Sometimes known as the limbic system, it represents twenty percent of the brain by volume and is partly responsible for emotions, sleep, attention, body regulation, hormones, sexuality, sense of smell, and production of many brain chemicals. However, noted American Neuroscientist, Joseph LeDoux,[6] contends that there is no real

---

[6] LeDoux, J. E. (1993). Emotional memory systems in the brain. *Behavioural Brain Research, 58*(1–2), 69–79.

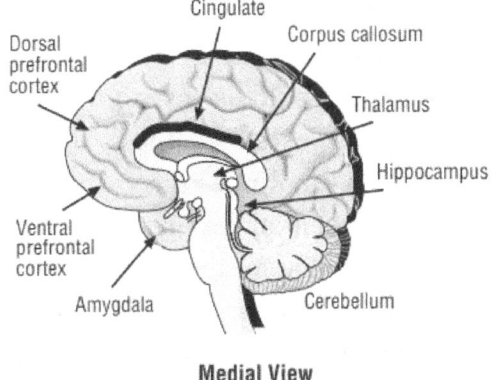

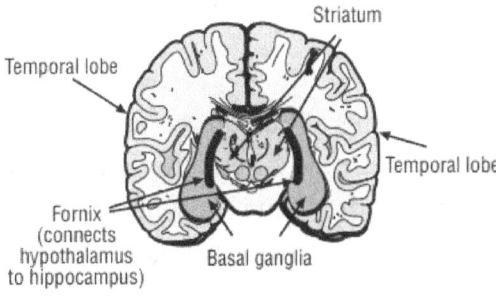

Figure 2: Medial and coronal views of the brain.

"limbic system," only specific structures that process emotion, such as the amygdala. In either case, this middle area of the brain, along with the parts of the cortex, helps you feel what you feel about the world.

The location of the brain area that allows you to know that you are "you" (consciousness) is disputed. British Neuroscientist Francis Crick[7] disputes that it may be dispersed throughout the

---

[7] Crick, F. (1994). *The Astonishing Hypothesis: The Scientific Search for the Soul*. New York: Charles Scribner's Sons.

cortex, or it may be in the thalamus, or it may be located near the reticular formation, a structure atop the brain stem. You'd think that this part of the brain would be easy to find — just cut away brain areas until a person loses awareness, right? But, it is not just a simple case of Jack the Ripper meets the Nutty Professor. Remember, the second essential feature of the brain is integration or *strong connectivity*. That means many areas connect to and influence other portions, so that specific sections of the brain may contribute separately and collectively to your sense of self. As Jensen would put it, one critical quality that makes the brain work so well is its degree of connectivity, not its individual structures.

When we are talking about the connectivity of the human brain, it is worth mentioning here that adolescence is the age when connectivity speeds up and the youth go through the phase of more thinking, rationalizing, sensing, deciding, etc.

Jay Giedd and his team[8] at the National Institute of Mental Health (NIMH) in 1999 revealed that rather than leaving childhood with a brain ready to take on the responsibilities of young adulthood, teens have to contend with a brain that is destroying old neural connections and building new ones. This compound study will forever alter how educators and parents interpret the mysterious behaviors of adolescents.

The above study highlights the following key points of the growing adolescent's brains:

---

[8] Giedd, J., Blumenthal, J., Jeffries, N., Castellanos, F., Liu, H., Zijdenbos, A., Paus, T., Evans, A., & Rapoport, J. (1999). Brain development during childhood and adolescence: A longitudinal MRI study. *Nature Neuroscience, 2,* 861–863.

1. The brain starts building new neurons and their connections.
2. The logic and wisdom building part of the brain develops a bit later than the part that deals with emotions and passions. That is why Sheryl Feinsein, author of the *Secrets of Teenage Brain*,[9] says that "teens are navigating a cerebellum hurricane without a compass."

How do these two points help us in understanding adolescent behavior and thoughts?

1. New Neurons and Connections

The human brain is made up of two cells:

Glial Cells: These work like glue because they connect other cells with each other and form 90 percent of the total brain.

Neurons: These cells constitute the other 10 percent of the brain.

Neurons are related to learning. They hold the secrets of the mind. Neurons communicate with the body and strike up "conversations" all over the brain. Their job is to coordinate ideas, feelings, and thoughts. They work at a very high speed, which is why you find adolescents are quite fast in their actions and reactions.

Neurons are made of a cell body, dendrites, and one axon. Dendrites, hair-like branches emerging from the plump cell body, receive information from other neurons. Each time an individual has a new experience or gains new information, one connection is made.

---

[9] Feinstein, S. G. (Ed.). (2009). *Secrets of the Teenage Brain: Research-based Strategies for Reaching and Teaching Today's Adolescents*. Corwin, 2455 Teller Road, Thousand Oaks, CA 91320: Corwin Press.

This helps us understand that adolescents are fast learners and the impact of the environment around them is deep on their brains. Hence, you can see that adolescents growing in troubled families under abusive parents learn to abuse both verbally and physically.

Another important thing that we learn about the adolescents here is that they can spend a large phase of their adolescent years in a specially designed environment in order to help them learn way more useful behavior.

The brain's ability to network and connect increases when dendrite receptors increase. Usually, a neuron's average number of dendrites is one thousand. However, one neuron can have many more dendrites.

Without mental stimulation, dendrites, connections between brain neurons that keep information flowing, shrink or disappear altogether. In Figure 3, it shows a stimulated brain from birth. A learning brain. An active life improves dendrite

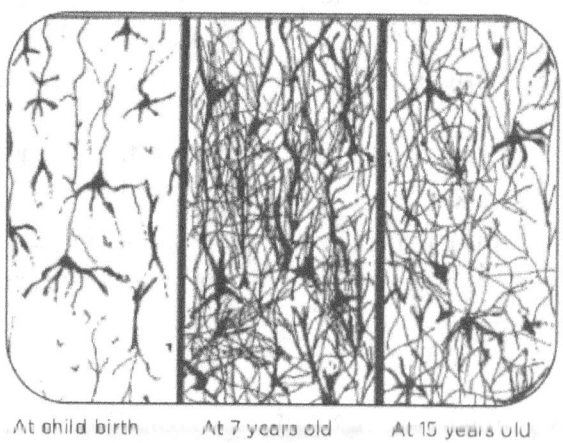

Figure 3: Images of neuronal connections in a learning child's brain.

networks and also increases the brain's capacity to regenerate; this is known as plasticity.

At a time when neurons are generating and increasing, there are certain habits or activities in the life of adolescents or in their environment that can inhibit the growth of neurons.

This is a very sensitive fact that we should understand 100 percent if we want to keep our youth productive and growing into positive humans as much as possible.

Activities that inhibit the growth of neurons are stress, shock, fear, violence, etc. The adolescents who spend their time badly fearing the numerous authorities around them, for example, suffer from inhibited growth of neurons. It is the same in the case of violence. Adolescents who are involved in violence either when they get violent or the adults get violent with them suffer from neuron damage and inhibition of growth of new neurons.

Alcohol is one of the substances that harm the growth of neurons. Eric Jensen in his book highlighted that scientists differ on what our daily net gain or loss in brain cells might be, "… and we know that certain behaviors affect the loss of brain cells. For example, although there's no evidence that an occasional glass of wine or beer destroys brain cells, it's clear that alcoholism does substantial damage."

These are just a few examples. Extreme sadness, bad accidents, huge losses, etc., also affect the brain negatively.

The extreme opposite of these things also damages the brain. The experts agree that a comfortable life, in the long run, can make the brain dull and unproductive.

It is the ability to face challenges and to come out of one's comfort zone that helps one learn more and more. Hence, the learning process encourages stronger brain connectivity and stronger brain growth.

So, staying in your comfort zone means staying away from your enhancement zone. The willingness to accept new challenges and to seek novelty as we mentioned above means we are constantly renewing our brain.

The dendrites are a hair-like structure, which extend like branches. These dendrites extend longer in order to enable the neurons to connect strongly at times of learning and facing new challenges. So, the process of learning allows these dendrites to extend like long tree branches and not remain stunted in their growth like stubby bushes.

2. Logic and Wisdom Build Later

The second point was about the brain part that deals with logic and wisdom. In fact, this part takes a bit longer in building and becoming large enough to process thoughts and actions on a rational basis. That is why we find that adolescents experience the spark of emotions earlier than being logical about things.

How does this information help us?

While dealing with youth at different paths of life like teaching, parenting, mentoring, coaching, and treating, we need to keep focused on their physical capability to learn and rationalize things. Taking an emotional approach is good in order to make training, coaching, and parenting more acceptable.

If the youth are unable to rationalize the importance of staying away from drugs or forming gangs from a logical point of view, we can pull them closer to us through our company, love, and care. Hence, our words will make more sense to their hearts and it will be easier for them to stay away from something which will make you sad and eventually hurt them emotionally.

Parents also need to understand the same that the youth need their love more than scolding, their company more than loneliness, emotional bonds more than logical reasons, etc. Parents take the route of logic quite early when their child's brain is not fully developed and the limbic section is unable to connect to logic. Hence, the teenage kid is unable to respond to them as they expect.

Here, a question pops up — Can the adolescents learn and understand while the part of their brain dealing with logic is not yet fully developed?

The answer is yes! The youth can learn things well because their short-term memory starts developing.

Feinsein,[10] in her book the *Secrets of Teenage Brain*, particularly highlighted a study done by researchers at the University of Colorado. The study revealed that the cortex finds patterns, integrates information, and attempts to give structure to information (the important stuff); the hippocampus deals with facts and details (rote memory). From this, it was inferred that the hippocampus memorizes and the cortex learns.

---

[10] *Ibid.*

She further highlighted that, like the rest of the brain, the hippocampus creates new dendrites and synapses during adolescence, which increases short-term memory in teenagers. Instead of just five to seven bits of information, teens may now be able to remember seven to nine bits. She calls it the information super highway! Feinsein elaborated as follows:

> *After synapses are generated in the brain, myelin a fatty substance made of glial is produced to insulate the neurons. Myelin covers the axons of neurons and enables information to travel efficiently. Myelinated tissue is referred to as white matter. The more extensive the myelination of axons, the faster information flows between the cells.*
>
> *At the same time, the ability to use symbolism, metaphors, and analogies increases in older adolescents. They are able to appreciate irony and sarcasm; their sense of humor becomes more sophisticated, and teachers often find themselves the objects of this increased capability.*
>
> *The adolescent is ready to hypothesize, create abstractly, and comprehend complex math theorems. The rampant changes are dynamic and undeniable. The transition from the childhood brain to the adolescent brain is like paving a gravel road with asphalt; teens are on their way to becoming faster, sleeker thinking machines. Their steadfast memory, jaunty step, thinking processes, language skills, and emotions all benefit from this smoother ride.*

Construction occurs throughout the teen brain. The parietal lobes (which process and desegregate sensory information like sights, sounds, and smells), temporal lobes (which process language and emotional behavior), occipital lobes (which process visual information), cerebellum (which processes coordination and thinking skills), and hippocampus (seat of short-term memory) all benefit from the overproduction and pruning of synapses.

When Giedd[11] moved to the University of California, Los Angeles (UCLA), to the Laboratory of Neuro Imaging, his team discovered that the parietal lobes did not complete the creation of gray matter until about the age of twelve and only then did they start pruning. Temporal lobes limped even further behind — they did not finish growing gray matter or begin the processes of pruning and myelination until the age of sixteen! In some areas, pruning and myelination follow even later. The brain does not release myelin to all neurons at the same time but rather in stages. The timing of the release of myelin appears to be dependent upon the developmental age of the individual, environment, and genetics. One of the last parts of the brain to receive myelin is the frontal cortex, the area responsible for abstract thinking, language, and decision-making. As the brain's frontal lobes become myelinated during adolescence, teens develop the ability to hypothesize, look into the future, deduct, analyze, and logically reason.

SUMMARY

1. When parents begin to appreciate how *adaptable, integrated,* and *sophisticated* their adolescents' brains are, the better they are able to intentionally and effectively engage their kids to bring about more desired behaviors.
2. Connectivity speeds up in adolescents' brains; they go through the phase of more thinking, rationalizing, sensing,

---

[11] *Ibid.*

deciding, etc. The brain starts building new neurons and connections.
3. The logic and wisdom building part of the adolescents' brain develops a bit later than the part that deals with emotions and passions.
4. Activities that inhibit the growth of neurons in adolescents' brains are stress, shock, fear, violence, etc. The adolescents who spend their time fearing the numerous authorities around them suffer from inhibited growth of neurons.
5. The transition from the childhood brain to the adolescent brain is like paving a gravel road with asphalt; teens are on their way to becoming faster, sleeker thinking machines.
6. One of the last parts of the brain to receive myelin is the frontal cortex, the area responsible for abstract thinking, language, and decision-making.
7. As the brain's frontal lobes become myelinated during adolescence, teens develop the ability to hypothesize, look into the future, deduct, analyze, and logically reason.

Chapter 4

Youth Brain — Part 2

In this chapter, we are going to dive deeper into specifically two areas of the brain, namely, the prefrontal cortex (PFC) and the limbic system. In the previous chapter, I alluded to this toward the end when I discussed "logic and wisdom build later."

I gave the example that if the youth are unable to rationalize the importance of staying away from drugs or forming gangs from a logical point of view, we can pull them closer to us through our company, love, and care. In fact, our words will make more sense to their hearts and it will be easier for them to stay away from something which will make you sad and eventually hurt them emotionally.

There is an explanation for this, and I call it the Clash of the Mind and Heart!

When we talk about the Clash of the Mind and Heart, we are essentially talking about a clash between cognitive development and emotional development. The "clash" naturally exists because these two aspects of development are not parallel in the physical maturation rate.

Researchers compare magnetic resonance images of teenagers and adults to prove how cognitive development does not happen at the same time with emotional development in adolescents.[1]

When the images of adults' brain were taken under the condition of fear, both the limbic area of the brain, emotion center, and the prefrontal cortex, judgment and reasoning center, were equally enhanced. Meanwhile, in the adolescents' brain, the same images displayed the limbic area enhanced, with the prefrontal cortex showing no activity. This is evidence for early development of emotions.

This is the reason why we experience that the "mind and heart" of the adolescents are constantly "clashing" during their teenage years — parents want them to, say, study hard, but they would rather hang out with their friends, sometimes even at the expense of their sleep or examination results. Why? Let's dive into this further.

PREFRONTAL CORTEX

This is the part of the brain that is primarily responsible for impulse control, forward planning, consequences consideration, and decision-making.

This is the "Seat of Executive Thinking," otherwise known as the "Brakes." If you place your right palm on your forehead, the

---

[1] Yurgelun-Todd, D. (2007). Emotional and cognitive changes during adolescence. *Current Opinion in Neurobiology, 17*(2), 251–257.

PFC resides just there. The PFC is primarily responsible for the following four functions:

- impulse control,
- forward planning,
- consequences consideration,
- decision-making.

Research shows that the PFC can "control" or regulate the rapid and impulsive processing of the limbic system gradually from childhood to adulthood.[2] This means that the impulsivity associated with the immature PFC development will slowly diminish. It is important to note that the PFC is fully developed around the age of 25 years old.[3]

Risky behavior and emotional reactivity in adolescents are the products of a biologically driven imbalance between increased novelty and positive sensation seeking in conjunction with immature "self-regulatory competence," which is the ability to calm down and consider consequences, before deciding on a more appropriate behavior to respond.

I recall an encounter I had with an angry teenager called Ben. I was getting ready to start a session with a class of teenage boys at a local secondary school. It was after mid-day recess, and the boys were strolling back into the classroom after the school bell rang. The bell signals the end of their recess time.

---

[2] Blakemore, S. J., & Choudhury, S. (2006). Development of the adolescent brain: implications for executive function and social cognition. *Journal of Child Psychology and Psychiatry, 47*(3–4), 296–312.

[3] Giedd, J. N. (2015). The amazing teen brain. *Scientific American, 312*(6), 32–37.

Almost everyone was back in class. Ben appeared at the back of the classroom, stood at the door, and looked into the classroom, with his head turning left and right skimming the entire class with his wide-open eyes, seemingly trying to look for someone.

Ben was a huge boy, slightly on the plump side, his face expressing his full rage, obviously angry at someone, and ready to pounce on the classmate that he was intently looking for at that point in time.

And, true to my assessment of his entire disposition, when Ben's eyes caught sight of this one boy sitting diagonally across the classroom from where he was, Ben clenched his fists really tightly, raised it up to slightly at his chest level, and started storming into the classroom. The boy that Ben was aiming for was sitting about two arms' lengths from where I was standing in front of the class.

Ben was pushing himself past all the tables and chairs that were in his way, and almost hyperventilating at the same time, breathing in and out very fast, getting ready to scream his lungs out at the boy angrily when he reached the front, and even possibly throwing a punch.

Being trained in martial arts and defense tactics, my instant reaction was to walk straight at him, trying to establish eye contact with him, and lunge with my arms stretched out from my side at his chest. Ben's eyes were dead fixed on his classmate, and he was not responding to my instructions to stop.

The moment my chest landed on his chest, I quickly used my body weight to push him toward the front entrance of the classroom. The entrance was on the same side of the classroom as the door by which he had stood trying to scan for his classmate earlier. By this time, Ben was already three-quarters of the way through from where he started, one table short of reaching his classmate. Once again, my instinct proved right. Ben threw a punch at his friend, but was stopped by my body-block during the lunge.

Once Ben was out of the classroom, I was not able to calm him down. So, I sought assistance from another teacher and managed to bring Ben down to the Principal's office. After about 10–15 minutes when Ben was calmer, I managed to process the incident with him.

At the moment when Ben appeared at the back of the classroom in rage and anger, what do you think was going on in his mind? Would Ben have thought about how he would want to express his emotions? Would he have considered his options before deciding what to do with the anger, let alone consider the consequences of his actions?

I found out later that Ben was made fun of during recess while playing with his friends, and there was one particular classmate who was allegedly the instigator, which led the rest to join in the fun. Ben was the victim of bully, and he was trying to take matters into his own hands by seeking revenge.

Chances are that in the moment, the teenager may not think twice about his or her actions, due to the immature "self-regulatory competence" or developing PFC. Studies have shown how children with deficits in this area are at higher risk of school failure, dropping out, drug use, violence, and crime.

Teenagers look old enough to understand complicated issues and find the logic behind them. But, the reality is that while their appearance is adult, their brains are not as old and mature as we expect. The development of the PFC is slow, but it keeps on competing with time. The experts explain that the prefrontal cortex has an active and significant role in youth maturation.

The red part in Figure 1 is the PFC. By looking at this image, you can understand that the human brain develops from back to front. Once the process of completion starts from behind, it continues until the last part of the brain.

What about children? Do they have functional prefrontal cortices?

In fact, the physical brain part is there, but it is the full "development", the neuro-connections for full cognitive functioning, that will continue to take place in the brain until they reach the adult age.

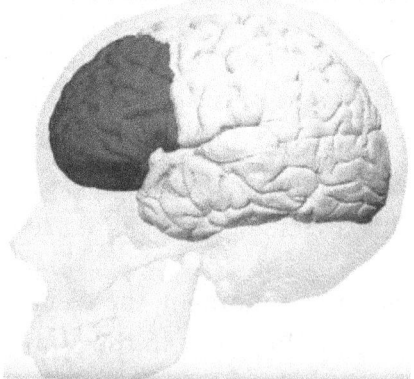

Figure 1: Prefrontal Cortex

There are two factors that can push the development and growth of the prefrontal. So, the planning skill and decision-making ability grow early. These two factors are experiences and stimuli. Children who go through a wide variety of challenges and thought-provoking motivations develop faster and become mature earlier.

ROLE OF THE PREFRONTAL CORTEX

There are several other functions that are included in the prefrontal cortex:

- Complex behavior coordination and keeping the complex actions coherent and in proper sequence.
- Control of desires and keeping them within the realm of different logical measures.
- Organization and control of emotional reactions.
- Personality grooming, development, etc.
- Organizing attention for most needed areas and keeping it distributed according to when and where it is needed.
- Increasing focus.
- Planning complex matters.
- Mentally weighing different matters and handling simultaneous information according to the priorities.
- Managing focus with a power of pushing away the distractions.

PARTS OF THE PREFRONTAL CORTEX

The PFC is naturally divided into several distinct parts according to its function.

Dorsolateral Prefrontal Cortex

This is the topmost part of the PFC. It manages overall cognitive processes like cognitive flexibility, planning, and managing memory.

This area specializes in problem-solving and directing and maintaining attention to a task, and this is the part that manages multitasking, too.

When our mental focus is on what we are doing at the moment and is happening now, our active memory is engaged with the dorsolateral prefrontal cortex (DLPFC), but it also connects to the hippocampus for retrieving and consolidating long-term clear memories.

A dysfunction in this area due to a traumatic incident may lead to issues with working memory, meting out in the hippocampus, long-term memory, as well as the combination of emotions with verbal expressions. This is a memory deficit which is linked to post-traumatic stress disorder (PTSD) because of an underactive left DLPFC.

Other DLPFC dysfunctions can be obvious in the form of alertness and attention deficit. Hence, it is apparent in the inability to preserve sufficient attention on a task from start to completion. Like other brain regions, the dorsolateral prefrontal cortex has some significant hemispherical differences. So, the left DLPFC is in association with approach behaviors, while the right is more associated with avoidant behaviors.

The Ventromedial Prefrontal Cortex

This part of the PFC helps us take new decisions with information taken in the form of a bigger picture from links to the ventral segmental area, amygdala, olfactory system, temporal lobe, and the thalamus.

Orbitofrontal Cortex

This part has a lot of functions similar to DLPFC. It is involved in the intellectual processing of decision-making, but because of its strong relation to the limbic system, it is specially associated with the decision-making ability built on emotional information. The orbitofrontal cortex (OFC) also works in regulating emotions and forming social attachments.

This region can be considered a junction for emotional and sensory information, efficiently integrating internal and external worlds. This part processes social information and incorporates it, thus helping with our interactions and perceptions. The OFC has another important role and that is the interpretation of several multifaceted social interactions. One example is the ability to understand or crack a joke.

Predicting the behavior of others and shaping up our behavior according to that is also the job of the OFC. Compared with other parts of the prefrontal cortex, the OFC has semi-circular differences. Hence, the left side deals with positive emotions and the right side deals with negative emotions.

Ventromedial Prefrontal Cortex

This part takes decisions of matters of a bigger picture obtained through connections with the temporal lobe, amygdala, thalamus olfactory system, and ventral segmental area. The connections in this part are quite strong. It is very well connected; it receives and sends bunches of information to different parts of the brain, especially the amygdala. Another function of the ventromedial prefrontal cortex (vmPFC) is to regulate emotions in specific social situations.

Overall, this part has the functions of making social and personal decisions along with the capability of learning from our mistakes. Hence, we judge different situations and allow our emotions to blend in with our ability to make decisions in this part of brain. Stimulation of the vmPFC is also linked with compassion, suppression of negative emotions, courage, guilt, and shame.

This brief study of the PFC parts and functions enables us to be clear about the development of the brain. The different functions of the PFC that we have just read mean a great deal in the life of every individual.

However, the most important part of this section remains the fact that adolescents experience the full development of the PFC around their mid-twenties. Before that time, most of their actions are based on their emotional understanding of matters.

This is the key point here that in our dealings and training of youth, we need to focus on their emotional side more as it is active and better developed at an early age. Expecting too much of logic and mature decisions from adolescents is unfair.

Several behavior patterns and reactions of teens are quite out of this world for us. We think of them as absurd, unreasonable, unfair, and most of the times inconsiderate. Actually, we are quick to put the blame on them and mostly we pick negative judgments and remarks to show our disagreement with their behavior.

In fact, if we fairly look at the behavior of adolescents with a proper understanding of their developing brain, we will find that they react spontaneously toward life and other humans. They act as their intuition directs them. They do not fake it for any reason negative or positive.

LIMBIC SYSTEM

The other area of the human brain that we need to know is the limbic system. This emotional motor system is responsible for the experience and expression of emotions. It is located in the core of the human brain, and deals with four key functions: emotions, memories, learning, and arousals (or stimulation). Eric Jensen pointed out the following[4]:

> "The territory in the middle of the brain includes the hippocampus, thalamus, hypothalamus, cingulate, basal ganglia, fornix, striatum, and amygdala. You could call this area both the chemistry lab and the drama department of the brain. It represents 20 percent of the brain by volume and is partly responsible for emotions, sleep, attention, body regulation,

---

[4] Jensen, E. (1998). *Teaching with the Brain in Mind*. Alexandria, VA: Association for Supervision and Curriculum Development.

hormones, sexuality, sense of smell, and production of many brain chemicals. However, noted neuroscientist Joseph LeDoux contends that there is no real "limbic system," only specific structures that process emotion, such as the amygdala. In either case, this middle area of the brain, along with the parts of the cortex, helps you feel what you feel about the world."

You can tell that the *Mind* refers to the PFC functions and the *Heart* refers to the limbic functions. They are broadly the rational and emotional parts of us that develop at different rates when we grow up, particularly during the adolescence period (see Figure 2).

Actually, the limbic system is the part of our brain that is involved in our emotional and behavioral responses, especially when our behavior is more concerned with our need for survival like having babies, caring for our loved ones, feeding, and fighting.

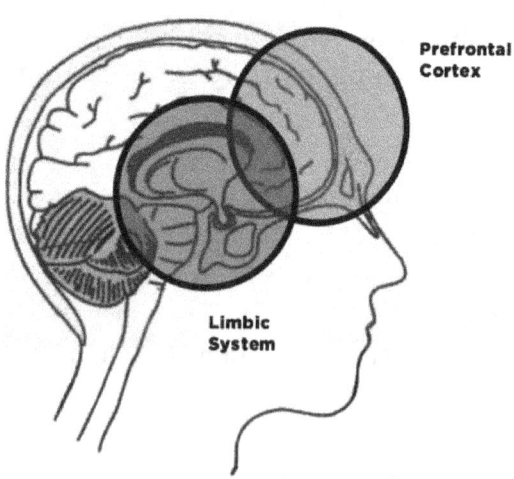

Figure 2: Limbic System and Prefrontal Cortex of Human Brain.

So, the limbic system is the *Seat of Emotions*, otherwise known as the "Survival Instinct Center." It works extremely fast and its connection with our motor responses develops very early in life. This is the reason why actions follow strong feelings in kids. It promotes survival.

There are essentially four parts in the limbic system: Thalamus, Hippocampus, Hypothalamus, and Amygdala.

The **Thalamus** is the relay station for incoming signals. It regulates all incoming signals before relaying them to other parts of the brain. An example could be the young person watching his friend plays his favorite online game, and that visual signal is relayed to the memory.

The **Hippocampus** is the memory bank, the place where meaning is encoded. The sight of his friend playing his favorite online game could evoke a positive accompaniment of friends or the hounding concerns of parents. Such mental images could conjure up memories of enjoyment with classmates or negative experiences with parents reacting over the use of the computer, respectively. The hippocampus would be responsible for calling up these memories to consciousness.

The hippocampus makes connections that associate our memories with a different sense. The example is the association of gingerbread aroma with the Christmas festivities. This part of the brain has a role in our ability to have 3D orientations or navigate the world.

The hippocampus is unique in generating new neurons from adult stem cells. This process is famous by the name of neurogenesis and is fundamental to one sort of brain plasticity. So, we can conclude that for learning new things, this is a key brain structure.

The **hypothalamus** is the hormone control center. It regulates body functions like sleep, sex, and eating through hormone control. At the puberty age, in particular, hormones like testosterone, estrogen, and progesterone are in full effect, and they can affect moods quite significantly. These three hormones are technically found in everyone, but in different proportions. Each of them has a unique function.

The hypothalamus is the primary node and works as the output of the limbic system; it has several important connections. It is connected with the septal nuclei, frontal lobes, and the brain stem in a net-like formation through the medial forebrain section. It also gets inputs from the amygdala and the hippocampus through the fornix. The connection takes place through two pathways: stria terminalis and ventral amygdalofugal. The hypothalamus is actively involved in some key functions like endocrine function, sexual function, and behavioral function. It also manages involuntary control of actions and physical movements.

As it performs several different functions which are highly necessary for humans, the hypothalamus needs inputs from the body.

There are inputs from most of the body as well as from the sense of smell, the retina, and the viscera. It is equipped with internal sensors for osmolarity, temperature, sodium concentration, and glucose.

With sensitive receptors for several signals inside the body, the hypothalamus deals with hormones, particularly steroid hormones, along with other hormones like leptin and orexin. It also deals with internal signals.

Some other important functions in the body are also under the direct influence of the hypothalamus, including normal behavior, autonomics, and endocrine functions. Endocrine functions are more essential for the body and therefore the hypothalamus controls them directly through axonal connections to the posterior pituitary gland or releasing factors into the hypothalamic–hypophyseal portal system. To activate the sympathetic nervous system, the hypothalamus uses its localized areas. There are also forecasts to the reticular formation elaborated in certain behaviors, especially emotional reactions.

Some functions are fundamental to the hypothalamus. These include functions that need a direct response like osmolarity regulation and temperature. The hypothalamus monitors many other functions directly like the internal milieu; hence it produces a regulatory response. In this way, it controls our appetite and the endocrine tasks.

It is worth mentioning here that there is the ventromedial nucleus inside the hypothalamus, which is considered a satiety area, while the sideways hypothalamic area is the center for feeding.

The complex behaviors related to human emotions are also designed by the hypothalamus, like sexual responses. The preoptic area of the hypothalamus is the place of greatest sexual dimorphism (difference in the arrangement between the sexes) and, by the side of the septal nuclei, there is an area of gonadotropin which releases the hormone projecting to the median eminence area of the hypothalamus. These sexual reactions include endocrine, autonomic, and behavioral responses.

Finally, the nucleus of the neuron clusters receives direct retinal response. This nucleus is responsible for controlling and arranging the circadian rhythms to the cycle of day–night.

We discuss now the hypothalamus' role in dealing with the following hormones:

Estrogen is usually thought of as a "female" hormone. In girls, it is made in the ovaries, adrenal glands, and fat cells and its levels are higher in those who are of reproductive age. In boys, small amounts of estrogen are made as a by-product of testosterone conversion.

In boys, **testosterone** is produced in the testicles, and to a lesser degree, in the adrenal glands. It helps build muscle tone, increases energy, contributes to a healthy libido, and aids in sperm production. Levels decline with age and with high stress in the body. Healthy levels are also important in women. Testosterone is produced in the female ovaries and a small amount is made in the adrenal glands.

Progesterone is a softening and nurturing hormone in the body. It helps balance the effects of estrogen on both the males' and females' bodies. Its calming effects help lift the mood and encourage restful sleep.

At puberty, adolescents are experiencing the full effect of the works of their hormones in their body. As a result, it is a time of increased emotional reactivity. Depending on how adults assist to regulate the teenagers, the emotional reactivity and sensitivity may play a role in higher incidence of affective disorder onset and addiction during this developmental period.

The **Amygdala** (otherwise known as the alarm system) is essentially the place where memories are assigned emotional meanings. To use the example of a boy watching his friend play his favorite online game, he recalls how his parents cautioned him about the use of the computer, especially when he has not completed his homework. He can either feel afraid because his parents might reprimand him or feel angry because his parents are often restrictive. He could be alerted to either take flight or fight. It is important to note that the amygdala has been implicated as a key neural region in emotional dysregulation in psychiatric disorders. This region is essential to learning the emotional significance of cues in the environment.

Not only this, the amygdala makes mutual connections within several brain areas like the thalamus, septal nuclei, orbital frontal cortex, hypothalamus, parahippocampal gyrus, cingulate gyrus, hippocampus, and brain stem. The one exception is the olfactory bulb which is the only part that inputs to the amygdala and does not get a mutual projection from the amygdala.

The amygdala is a vital center for organizing behavioral, endocrine, and autonomic responses to environmental incentives, including the emotional content. In the amygdala, it is important to coordinate responses to stress and integrate many behavioral reactions like anxiety and stress including the survival of a person or his kind. Injuries of the amygdala decrease the ability to respond to some emotions like stress, but in particular is its response to conditioned emotions. Motivating amygdala helps in the arousal of several like rage. Hence, the amygdala responds to a variety of emotional stimuli, but mostly those related to fear and anxiety.

These four brain parts of the limbic system make up the Center of Emotions. To understand the behaviors of young persons, it is imperative to know the general functions of this Center of Emotions. It is important to note also that the limbic system is fully developed between the ages of 10 and 15 years.

APPLYING WHAT WE LEARN

With this study of the human brain's development and the clear difference between the part that is linked to logic and the part that is linked to emotions, we are able to understand several facts about adolescents. As parents, educators, mentors, and coaches, we need to know the brain and it matters to us.

> "Many studies present enough clear and solid information to be transformed into classroom practice. In his book, Minds, Brains, and Learning, James Byrnes suggests that any ideas from neuroscience that we want to implement should be integrated and consistent with other models from psychology and behavioral sciences. This is a good approach."
> — Eric Jensen

There are some key points that we need to highlight here. After studying the difference between the two parts of the brain, one of which is linked to the brain and another to the heart, we need to focus on certain behavioral traits of adults toward adolescents:

- Although emotions grow at a younger age and develop faster than logic, adolescents can develop their behavior step by step into a fully reformed personality faster than we expect. This is possible when we support them with our positivity, love, and care.
- It is clear the late growth of the brain's logic part does not affect the behavior of youth deeply as the emotional part of the brain successfully handles many different functions in the body and regulates emotions to a great extent.
- Emotions are a powerful source of understanding. Like adolescents' capacities to touch, see, smell, hear, intuit, and think, their ability to feel is sufficient for their behavior with others and also self-awareness.
- Adults should give a chance to adolescents to talk about their emotions and express their feelings. This is one way that is highly positive and constructive in keeping them on the right track to a great extent.
- As parents and teachers, we do not need to get alarmed by every emotion our youth express to us. In fact, brain development is fast and it is bringing new changes and new connections in the different systems of the brain every day. Hence, the adolescents have a wide capacity to change and "mend" their thoughts that seem unproductive or useless to us.
- Feeling depressed and anxious happens quite often in adolescents because of the emotional changes that take place fast, and the kids try to deal with them on their own due to fear of reprehension, punishment, and judgment from the adults. That is why they do not share their disturbing feelings with

their parents and teachers because they feel insecure. They would rather find another young teenager to share their secrets and emotions with and bond with.
- The emotional changes are fast and many times the negative feelings overcome their minds and they feel lonely, neglected, unimportant, unloved, or useless. At such moments, the kids do not need a long lecture or a piece of advice, they need company and warmth of care. In fact, their developing brain will sort the things for them in a fine logical sense quite soon. So, you just stay positive because it will keep them strong and feeling good about themselves.
- Aggression is a normal emotional surge that happens due to brains developing connections. This emotion can be destructive if a young teenager is left alone with his emotions. He may attempt to commit suicide from his emotional surge that makes him feel alone, guilty, or worthless. Since the emotional part of the brain has already become active in the adolescents, we can keep them safe from going beyond normal during their aggressive spell.
- The study of brain development helps adults get rid of the misconceptions and myths that destroy their relationship with the youth.
- The neglect of the brain's condition and its development is a big mistake that leads to drastic results.
- Adolescence is a time for parents to get ready to stand next to their child in all the challenges that he is going to face.
- There is no reason for parents to feel frustration, anger, and hopelessness. They should also not put the blame on the adolescents and make them feel worse. In fact, adolescence is a time when the youth need encouragement and support.

EMBRACE THE JOURNEY MOVING FORWARD

The imbalance between the prefrontal and limbic responses is real and it is biological. The limbic system is fully developed during puberty at about 10–15 years of age. The prefrontal cortex, however, begins to develop during puberty and becomes fully mature only around the age of 20–25 years. **This is 10 years apart!**

Adolescents would instinctively react emotionally when their emotions are triggered. If they are angry, it is unlikely that their first response will be well considered. It is unlikely also that they would have thought of the consequences, deliberated on possible actions, and executed an action appropriately.

It would take about 25 years to develop the full PFC–limbic system neuronal network. It is especially important for parents to note that the window of opportunity for the development of the PFC–limbic neuronal network is from age 5 to adolescence.

The child will unconditionally seek positive sensational experiences or novelties. The drive to seek such experiences is naturally strong. It is often a limbic behavior. Deprivation of those experiences will lead the child to "fight." If the child were hungry, she would naturally seek food without any PFC interventions. If the child were angry, he may naturally express that emotion aggressively.

We can now appreciate better that in the seeking food or comfort when the child is hungry or angry, the child may not know that it is inappropriate to steal the food or hit someone else unless we help them learn.

The ability to learn is primarily a cognitive function. The cornerstone of cognitive development is the ability to suppress inappropriate thoughts and actions in favor of goal-directed ones, especially in the presence of compelling incentives.

Therefore, teaching a young person appropriate behavior in response to trying to experience a positive sensation needs to be done consistently over time, with compelling rewards to motivate the learning or the change. It also needs to be goal directed. Otherwise, the learning would be susceptible to interference from competing sources. Goal-directed behavior requires the control of impulses or the delay of gratification for optimization of outcomes, and this ability matures across childhood and adolescence.

The shaded area in Figure 3 reflects the window of opportunities for parents, educators, and youth workers to assist adolescents to develop the full PFC–limbic neuronal network. Some adults may consider this same period as a risky period because this is the period when adolescents are the most susceptible to negative and inappropriate resources.

Guided by the understanding of neurobiology, the brain is literally "under construction" during this period. Everything the child learns stimulates the growth of brain neurons. Therefore, teaching needs to be consistently engaging, so that the child is motivated to learn.

The more consistent the engagement is with the adolescent, by appealing more to the early development of the limbic system,

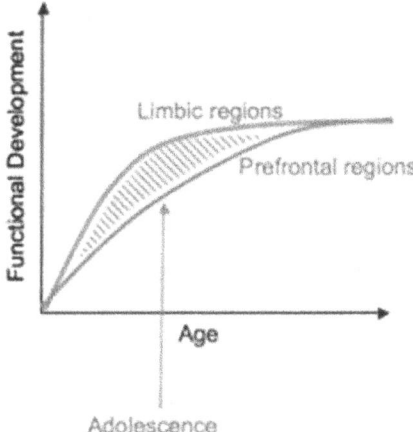

Figure 3: Development of the Prefrontal Cortex Together with the Limbic Regions, as a Function of Age.

the higher the chance for impulse control to develop in a more sustained way. This means that adolescents can be taught to control their impulse and delay their gratification, but it needs to be taught in a goal-directed fashion, appealing to the heart — the limbic system!

SUMMARY

1. Youth instinctively make emotional decisions as the limbic system — the emotional center — develops much earlier than the prefrontal cortex — the judgment and reasoning center.
2. The limbic system, comprising the thalamus, hippocampus, hypothalamus, and amygdala, manages four primary areas:
    i. Emotions,
    ii. Memories,
    iii. Learning,
    iv. Arousal/Stimulation.

3. The prefrontal cortex consists of the dorsolateral prefrontal cortex, ventromedial prefrontal cortex, orbitofrontal cortex, and ventromedial prefrontal cortex. It has four primary functions:
    i. Impulse control,
    ii. Forward planning,
    iii. Evaluating consequences,
    iv. Decision-making.
4. On average, the limbic system fully develops around 15 years of age, while the prefrontal cortex only fully develops about 25 years of age.
5. The prefrontal cortex can mature faster and earlier when children undergo a wide variety of challenges and thought-provoking motivations while being facilitated by their parents with positivity, love, and care.
6. Adolescence is a phase riddled with huge emotional changes and an influx of negative emotions. During this period, parents need to allow their youth to express and talk about their emotions. This helps develop a stronger bond of trust between the youth and the parents.
7. Teaching youth appropriate behaviors require goal-directed learning that engages the youth emotionally. Consistent rewarding is necessary to help them develop impulse control.

Chapter 5
It Takes a Village

Every time we talk about youth success, be it academic success, sports excellence, overcoming adversity, or facing challenges and rising above, have you wondered if the success and resilience displayed were achieved by the youth's own merit? No doubt most of the effort and even sacrifices were made by the young person, and it did not come without pain; is it the case then that the child himself or herself achieved the success alone?

In all my years of working with youth, especially those who are more at risk, for youth to succeed, it takes an entire village! Again, this may sound clichéd, but it is really not. There is an African saying fused with a Vietnamese saying that goes like this, "It takes a village to raise a child, but only a child to raze the village." To simply put it out there, if a child-athlete were to have achieved a professional standard of performance in swimming, he would have undergone not only hours of trainings in the pool with his coach but also hours of academic coaching with his tutor, encouragement from parents to turn up at trainings, visualization trainings with a psychologist to prepare for competitions, nutritionists to ensure the child is eating and being nourished well, doctors to medicate for sickness or for pain management, occupational therapists or physiotherapists for rehabilitation of injuries, and the list goes on. Get the picture?

For a child who has been physically abused, growing up being constantly beaten and threatened, always fearful and worried about what might happen every moment, how do you think he or she might even succeed in life? In the first place, if the child kept quiet about the abuse, would the child be helped in any way? In such a situation, it would take an attentive teacher in school, a counselor, or even a neighbor to notice micro-behaviors, injuries or marks, or commotion at home to launch some preliminary investigation. The investigation could be conducted by the school, a social service agency, or even the neighborhood police. Once the abuse is ascertained, possibly by legislation, the child could be removed from the family and made to reside in a rehabilitation center, or even fostered by other families. The child could be provided counseling services, made to undergo therapy, enrolled into community programs, provided educational support, and later reintegrated into the greater community. The list goes on, and it really depends on the situation that the child is in. Every child is different, and the needs vary significantly. These two examples may be extreme on both ends of the spectrum, but it is by no means any less resource intensive for a child in between this spectrum to succeed. The point being, it takes a village to raise a child!

At the same time, if all the said support and resources were not provided for the child-athlete or the abused child, what could have become of him or her? What would be the worst-case scenario? This discussion is not to stereotype any persons, behaviors, or families. If there were any resemblance of such, it is purely coincidental. A possible worst-case scenario could be that the child becomes resentful that he or she was not talent-spotted by a national team talent scout, and inflicts the same pain on others by spreading negative sentiments online, creating an uproar of negative social events; as for the abused child, he could have been abused so badly that he died or become a perpetrator himself, hurting not only his own family but also those he works with and those in the community — and it takes only "a child to raze the village."

URIE BRONFENBRENNER ECOLOGICAL SYSTEMS THEORY

The late Urie Bronfenbrenner, a Russian-born American psychologist, who is best known for his ecological systems theory, explained how individuals and their surrounding interact with each other to influence their growth and development. The theory focuses on the importance of looking at children and adolescents in multiple ecological systems to try to comprehend the development of the child. To follow the system closely, we can typically see that the adolescent is enmeshed in more than one system. It would typically commence from the most intimate care ecological system, usually the family or home, and move outward to the larger systems like the school, the community, the society at large, and the world. Every system will somehow come into contact with each other, and would be able to influence each other in the various aspects of the child's lives (see Figure 1).

Microsystem

This is the smallest, most intimate system in which adolescents live. It consists of the everyday home, grandparents' care, student

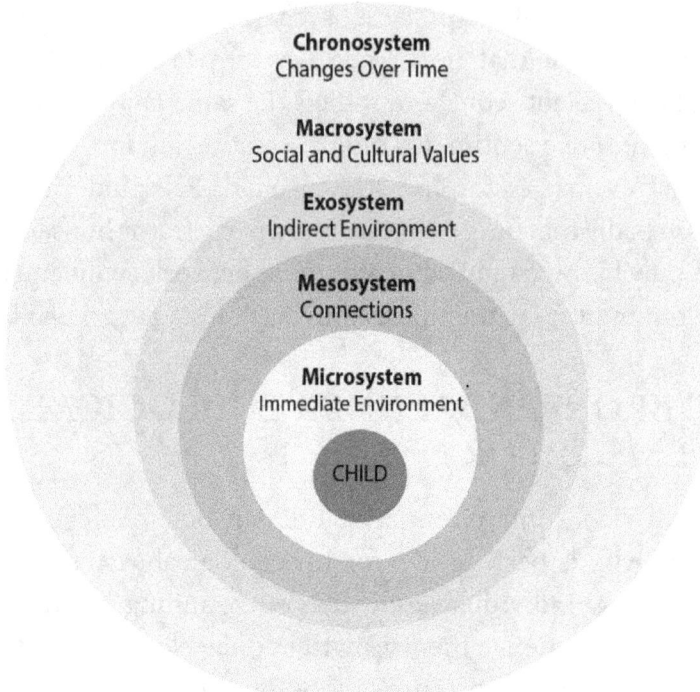

Figure 1: Bronfenbrenner's ecological systems theory.
Source: The Psychology Notes Headquarters https://www.PsychologyNotesHQ.com

care, school, and community environment of the youth. The interactions within this system usually involve intimate relationships with family members, caregivers, classmates, and teachers. How these people interact with the child will inevitably affect the growth and development of the child. This goes hand in hand with how the youth responds to these same people within this system, and how it is reciprocated. You can imagine that the more positive, supportive, empowering, and nurturing the interactions and relationships are, the more it would enhance the child's development.

Mesosystem

With this system, we are looking at the different microsystems that the adolescents are in, which are interacting with and influencing each other. These are like the connection between home and school, or between family and friends, or between family and community. For example, if parents are involved and welcomed in the relationships of their teens' social groups, and are constantly interacting and in touch with them, this would influence the child's growth in a positive way through a lot of mindshare and synchrony. The reverse is also true, if parents are constantly critical of their child's friends and expressed distaste about their behaviors or activities, the teenager may be conflicted emotionally and it may negatively impact the development of the child.

Exosystem

This system consists of the connections between systems that may not involve the development of the adolescent directly, but it does impact and influence them indirectly. Bronfenbrenner talks about people and places where adolescents are not party to the interactions directly and yet their lives are affected and influenced. Such people and places could include the workplaces of parents, extended families, and the neighbor communities. For example, parents may talk about their struggles in parenting their adolescents to people at work; they share and learn different parenting strategies from each other. When they reach home, they attempt or implement some applicable strategies on their child.

Macrosystem

This is the system that still has a significant influence on the adolescents, although the people and places are very distant from them. This system is huge and massive; it involves societal values, culture, traditions, heritage, even political and economic systems. An example of this could be children and adolescents in areas where there are wars or limited supplies of food and resources; the living experience and development of the kids would be very different from those in more peaceful or well-resourced environments.

Chronosystem

This final system provides the interplay of time across all systems, at the same time playing a critical role in influencing change in the adolescent's life. Change is the only constant here. In this system, change may happen within the family structures of the youth, their progress through education, parents' employment status and societal engagement, climate change and its impact on community resources, economic cycles, and even wars. When we look into all these systems, Bronfenbrenner's Ecological Systems Theory is able to help us appreciate how the adolescent's development is impacted and influenced by the interrelatedness of each system. It starts with the awareness of the situations that the adolescents are in before we can be attuned to the way adolescents behave in different circumstances. Take, for example, an adolescent who may be bullying other teens in school — he or she may be a victim of violence at home, a terrified one. With such variations, concerned adults who may be worried about the care of the youth should focus on his or her environment or system; this should include the quality and type of connections that are present between each system.

POSITIVE YOUTH DEVELOPMENT

Therefore, when we discuss positive youth development, it is with this understanding that we want to perceive, understand, and engage youth; we want to engage the various systems that the youth are in. With Bronfenbrenner's Ecological Systems Theory, it is actually inevitable that the systems would need to be engaged. However, it is precisely this inevitability that is not taken into consideration when we are talking about youth development, an approach that falls short of helping youth succeed or develop positively.

The United States Department of Health and Science Services defines Positive Youth Development as follows:

> "Positive youth development is an intentional, pro-social approach that engages youth within their communities, schools, organizations, peer groups, and families in a manner that is productive and constructive; recognizes, utilizes, and enhances young people's strengths; and promotes positive outcomes for young people by providing opportunities, fostering positive relationships, and furnishing the support needed to build on their leadership strengths."

They formulated the following equation:

$$PYD = \text{Positive Experience} + \text{Positive Relationships} + \text{Positive Environments}$$

PYD is an "intentional" and "pro-social" engagement approach, focused on the youth's strengths to help them achieve positive relationships and leadership within their communities!

The implication here then is that parents cannot do this alone; in fact, parents are unable to provide the positive experience, the positive relationships, and the positive environments that the adolescents need alone.

Parents often try to do so alone, thinking they can engage their teens better. While there are instances where this may be the case, more often than not parents can hardly manage them, let alone engage them. Those who recognize the need to engage the various systems, and do so intentionally, will find that their teenagers are often engaged, self-motivated, and self-directed.

We can understand this further by looking at the work of four researchers from Search Institute in the area of PYD, Peter Benson, Peter Scales, Stephen Hamilton, and Arturo Sesma Jr. They reviewed numerous studies and found that the following principles when understood and applied intentionally, led adolescents toward self-leadership:

1. All youth have the inherent capacity for positive growth and development.
2. All youth thrive when they are embedded in relationships, contexts, and ecologies that nurture their development.
3. All youth will be positioned for further positive growth when they participate in multiple nutrient-rich relationships, contexts, and ecologies.
4. All youth benefit from these relationships, contexts, and ecologies:

- Support, empowerment, and engagement are important developmental assets for all youth, generalizing across race, ethnicity, gender, and family income.
- However, the strategies and tactics for promoting these developmental assets can vary considerably as a function of social location.

1. Community is a viable and critical "delivery system" for positive youth development.
2. Youth are major actors in their own development and are significant (and underutilized) resources for creating the kinds of relationships, contexts, ecologies, and communities that enable positive youth development.

Knowing these principles will help us engage teenagers in a more "intentional" manner, and at the appropriate level of their interest and motivations.

For example, with the view that "youth are major actors in their own development," parents want to constantly and proactively look out for their child's strengths and facilitate "pro-social" engagements where they get the opportunity to act on they own without much parental interventions. This is so that they are able to build positive relationships with people with full autonomy and have the opportunity to lead positively in their respective communities.

Parents may find it daunting to apply the principles when they are trying to engage their teenagers. It can be quite counterintuitive. However, Assets Coming Together (ACT) for Youth has come up with a framework for you to use. The ACT for Youth Center for Community Action is supported by the New York

State Department of Health. The Center aims to connect research to practice in the areas of positive youth development and adolescent/young adult health. The following are the points of the framework:

1. **Focus on strengths and positive outcomes:** It is very easy to spot the wrongs of the teenager. It often happens too quickly. Instead, catch them doing good and affirm them for it. There is a difference between praise and affirmation. I praise when I say, "Good Job!"; I affirm when I say, "You were very helpful in carrying the books for the teachers! Good job!"
2. **Focus on the youth's voice and engagement:** It is very easy to think that youth contributions may not measure up to adult standards or expectations. In so doing, we remove their voice from the situation or the relationship, and they disengage over time. Instead, we want to invite their contributions no matter how insignificant it may be. The more we do so, the more they become engaged, and the higher the possibility that they can rise to the standards and expectations of adults. Not that they have to, they become more capable of doing so.
3. **Focus on strategies that involve all youth:** It happens in schools, communities, and even in families. The more "misbehaving" or "talented" child often gets the most attention and the most support. It could either be for counseling or gifted program, respectively. Not that specific needs should be neglected; in fact, it is critical for targeted interventions to be provided for those who need it. When that is provided, the overall strategy must be to level all youth upward together. This is when the communities become more involved and where the magic happens!

4. **Focus on community involvement and collaboration:** It follows from the preceding points that involvement with the community is necessary. This can be faith based. And, it goes beyond programs or services. When youth are involved in a community, they get the opportunity to find themselves, feel a sense of belonging, and do something meaningful. It also promotes organizational change and collaboration for greater good.
5. **Focus on long-term commitment:** It holds therefore that when youths are meaningfully engaged, they thrive! And, with continued support from all stakeholders within each system of the youth's life, the child could go on to become a very successful adult. If a child could then be assisted to work on the short- and long-term goals, and to commit to achieving those goals, success awaits him or her!

Doing all of the above then is taking the PYD perspective to view the adolescent years as full of potential rather than rife with problems to be solved. Instead of merely encouraging adolescents to avoid risky behaviors, PYD emphasizes strategies that enhance positive qualities that adolescents already possess. The approach views adolescents as having a lot to offer and promotes the idea that adults can make a significant and positive difference in young people's lives.

PYD then is a set of principles that can be applied to any settings or programs where young people spend time to increase the likelihood of positive outcomes. Using this approach provides young people with opportunities to build core skills that can support positive development across all areas of their lives. In fact, when parents or youth programs take or implement a PYD approach, research shows that it positively impact the youth's academic achievement, family relationships, mental health, and physical health.

SUMMARY

1. Helping youth succeed requires the engagement of their surrounding ecological systems. Based on Bronfenbrenner's Ecological Systems Theory, the systems that need to be involved are the microsystem, mesosystem, exosystem, macrosystem, and chronosystem of the youth.
2. PYD is an engagement approach that strives to help youth achieve positive outcomes and leadership in their communities. It is the accumulation of the positive experiences, relationships, and environments of the youth.
3. To engage the youth more successfully, parents can apply the ACT framework in their engagement practices:
    a. Focus on strengths and positive outcomes.
    b. Focus on the youth's voice and engagement.
    c. Focus on strategies that involve all youth.
    d. Focus on community involvement and collaboration.
    e. Focus on long-term commitment.

Chapter 6
Intentional Engagement

Now that we know how adolescents are like neurologically speaking, let's discuss its implications. Neurologically, we know now that adolescents are more "feelings based" than "logic based." They are blinded to logic when their emotions are fully engaged. They need timeouts to cool down and process their emotions. This does not mean that logic does not make sense to them, or they cannot be logical. They absolutely can. It can happen after the timeout.

Being more feeling based, adolescents go through the following changes:

- Strong feelings and intense emotions are apparent from their behavior on several occasions. The mood is often unpredictable. Though the increased emotional imbalance leads to confusion, the teenager soon learns how to control it and to express his emotions like a grown up.
- The adolescents become more sensitive toward emotions like anger of their adults.
- They start learning and understanding other people's emotions. With time, this ability becomes stronger, though

they might make a mistake several times in order to understand the facial expressions and body language of other adults.
- They become highly self-conscious about their appearance, style, and physical changes. Their good appearance lifts their morale and looking bad or old-fashioned makes them lose their confidence.
- The more they grow older, the more their self-consciousness increases and they compare their appearance and body with their peers.
- They develop an "unbeatable" state of mind when they think that they are unbeatable and no harm can come to them. As the decision-making part of the brain is still under development, they overlook what the consequences of their actions might be.
- Their logical development is still incomplete; that is why they easily follow the logic of anyone who they like or feel comfortable with. However, when they react to certain things on their own, their spontaneous reaction is based on the information that their limbic system considers and deliberates.

We find that parents may repeatedly scold their child to complete their homework first before playing computer games. Does the child not hear or understand his or her parents' explanations for the need to complete their homework first? Why then does he or she not comply? It is interesting to note here that parents would typically repeat their instructions or reprimand the child again, knowing that the child would still continue to play on the computer, especially when parents are not at home.

IS LISTENING TO OR COMPLYING WITH PARENTS' INSTRUCTIONS VERY DIFFICULT?

The problem with teens not listening to their parents is worldwide. Everywhere, parents are worried about this issue and the teens are extremely unhappy with their adults. In fact, the problem is two-sided.

Parents do not really understand what their troubled teenager wants. They have some thoughts of their own in their mind and they follow it. For example, a parent has a demanding job. He does not take any holidays or spend any quality time with his kids on weekends. He thinks that supplying cash and life necessities is what makes his kids happy.

On the other hand, the kids want to talk with him, spend some relaxing time with him. They are looking forward to some quality parenting. A few holidays from work and going for a picnic is what they want at the moment, but the parent thinks that this will cost him cash that should not be "wasted" on such an activity. He thinks that the kids go to school, spend time with their peers, and that is sufficient to make them happy.

This is just one example. There may be other reasons also for the increasing distance between parents and their kids. Parents may have very high expectations of their kids and pressures them to meet those expectations. This may frustrate them and lead to resentment. Their disobedience could be a screaming sign of either trying to manage parents' expectations, with the distancing being an attempt to avoid trying to meet those expectations, or feeling overwhelmed, possibly even breaking down, with their distancing being an attempt to run away for self-preservation. Either way, they may be screaming WHY SO MANY EXPECTATIONS?

Parents could have a mental picture of their child studying politics in Harvard or medicine at Cambridge. They may be putting all their effort into making this dream a reality, possibility even starting their preparation when the child was very young. And, all this time, they may not have considered if their growing child had any of his or her own dreams, interests, or aspirations. Every child is ambitious and when the adolescent period starts, he or she becomes more emotional about what he or she wants to do.

This gap between parent and child is known to widen as parents persistently stay firm in their choices, and the child becomes more inclined toward what he or she is interested in. So, the gap starts to become bigger for both parent and child.

The teens' activities are regarded by parents as "nonsensical" stuff, "not purposeful," "unproductive," or "unconstructive," which in essence means that it will not amount to anything that will help lead the teenager toward academic excellence, having meaningful engagement, or being surrounded by positive peer influence.

Controlling for all other factors, the child essentially wants to play computer games more compared to doing his or her homework first. This is because it is more fun, exciting, social, rewarding, relaxing, and even empowering sometimes. The positive impact of doing his homework first still cannot outweigh what he can achieve now in the games or with his friends the immediate gratification that gaming or being with friends provides and the heightened sense of overall well-being. Is this even logical? With guidance, reflection, and with the help of adults processing the instinctual limbic responses, young persons can learn to make more logical and sensible decisions and even delay gratification over time. It will take a while before the young person can fully self-regulate. Ten years is the guide!

This is not to say that the young person is unable to be rational or logical as mentioned earlier. They can do so with assistance, guidance, supervision, and support, especially the support to deal with their emotions, like sadness, anger, and frustration. These emotions can be overwhelming. Once they are supported, listened to, empathized with, and they feel attended to by the adult, they would then be more disposed to understand what the emotions are about, they would be more inclined to learn skills to handle or manage the emotions and situation better, and they would be more willing to learn the lessons that need to be taught, or reflect on the lessons that they learned through the experience, even listening to parents!

That said, there is another area which needs to be highlighted. Adolescents are going through a transitional phase of entering adulthood from childhood. This phase is all about emotional, cognitive, and psychosocial development. Cognitive development is marked with a clear phase of struggling to think like the adults do. This is observable in three different kinds of behaviors.

The first behavior is in teens trying to prove themselves as grown-ups and assuming that they understand the reason of things. They do not naturally have this ability in its full form, because we now know that their cognitive brain part is still developing. For example, a teenage girl may think she has all the good reasons to be out late at night with her friends drinking or availing herself physically and emotionally when a male requests for it to show her commitment and interest toward the relationship. In her view, it is logically fine!

Second, it is in their style of thinking. In actual fact, at this stage of development, adolescents start thinking abstractly. Their ability to imagine things is strong. They are able to imagine things that they have not actually experienced or even seen. We hear the common saying that youth are fearless or idealistic. This is it. The imagining takes the adolescents to a new level of thinking about feeling loved, braving adventures, embarking on entrepreneurship, advocating causes, and even pursuing spirituality. The reason is that the part of the brain that has started this developmental functioning happens very early in life, and it is where the occipital lobe is situated as well. This area is at the lower back part of the brain. It is in the visual cortex as well. So, the imagination is very strong in teenagers rather than the adults.

Related to this, with their strong imagination, adolescents experience **personal fable**. This term was coined by psychologist David Elkind in 1967 due to his work on the Egocentrism in Adolescence. Adolescents think that they are the center of attention, because they are so special and unique and that they have a certain audience who loves to watch them. Most of the time, this special audience is their peers! The personal fable develops from the thought that the imaginary audience is impressed by them and that is why they like to watch them.

According to Elkind, this intense focus on themselves as the center of attention is what ultimately leads to the belief that one is absolutely unique, and therefore, they feel completely invulnerable. The experts agree that although the adolescents are aware of the risks involved in many activities, they fail to restrict themselves from such risky activities. The two distinct features of personal fable are feelings of uniqueness and invulnerability. Elkind puts it this way, "the complex of beliefs in the uniqueness of (the adolescent's) feelings and of his or her immortality might be called "personal fable," a story which he or she tells himself or herself, and which is not true."

Neuroimaging studies have found that the adolescents may find stronger emotional satisfaction with risk-taking behavior. This satisfaction pushes them to be involved in risky activities. The adolescent may not be able to imagine and measure the consequences of any risky actions. One example is not taking care of themselves while being sick. They are simply not able to relate cause and result with regard to healthy behavior, for example, overeating, smoking, drugs, alcohol, reckless driving, or early sex. Since they find it satisfactory to be involved in risky behaviors, they are not prepared to stay away from the risks, for example, not using condoms, traveling with drunk drivers, or driving recklessly.

Before we talk about the third type of behavior of adolescents, we explain here what metacognition is. The following is the definition according to Wikipedia:

> "Metacognition is "cognition about cognition", "thinking about thinking", "knowing about knowing", becoming "aware of one's awareness" and higher-order thinking skills. The term comes from the root word "meta", meaning "beyond", or "on top of". Metacognition can take many forms; it includes

knowledge about when and how to use particular strategies for learning or problem-solving. There are generally two components of metacognition: (1) knowledge about cognition and (2) regulation of cognition."

Adolescents' thinking is sometimes characterized as a form of operational thinking, which is to think about thinking. This metacognition allows youth to develop an ability to think about what they are feeling or displaying and how others recognize them.

This thought occupies their brain and it mostly occurs during the teenage years of life. Youth think that everyone around them is noticing them, thinking of them, and mostly it is the other youth (the imaginary audience) that they imagine are thinking of them and noticing them.

This thinking behavior can have dire consequences. At times, adolescents fear to show their tiredness or illness to their peers, thinking they would not appreciate it. Hence, they hide their condition. The matter that is important here is the serious thoughts and imagination of the adolescents. They really think that their thinking is reality and there is an actual audience who is mindful of them.

With the discussion of these three observable traits of adolescents, stemming from the understanding of their cognitive development, we are now in a better position to appreciate youth more realistically. Otherwise, we will keep on blaming them or accusing them, instead of taking a more positive approach with them, which they essentially need and thrive on.

Adults in general may need to learn to appreciate the nature of the young person more, and be prepared to be there for him or her for the next 10 years of his or her life. Be prepared to do what? To help facilitate the connections between the limbic system and prefrontal cortex, by asking questions about and processing with the young person all their limbic responses.

The goal is to help them understand their limbic responses and to develop skills and strategies to deal with and manage them as they come along. It is safe to assume that almost every action from the young person, at the first instance, would be a limbic response. Therefore, the sooner adults appreciate this reality, the better they will be at managing young persons more intentionally and with greater effectiveness.

There is this saying when we work with teenagers — "When we limbically confront the emotionally charged teen, especially when he or she is dealing with negative emotions, the adult would always be at the losing end."

Essentially, if a student vents his anger by using expletives, and the teacher angrily reprimands him and demanded that he apologize for being disrespectful, there is a high chance that the student would be more angry, and the lesson on being respectful would have been lost right there — to angrily reprimand and demand compliance from the student, when he is angry, is considered a limbic confrontation; at the same time, the good intention to teach respect in that exchange is lost. If this approach persists, every good lesson would be lost, and the adult will continue to lose ground with the child.

Why is this so? The teen would not be able to rationalize and understand the adult's intentions, and the adult would only provoke the child more. If the adult wanted to sincerely teach the child a valuable lesson, his efforts would be futile.

Take a similar example of a teen in school having a bad day. He is angry about some incident that happened earlier that day. His teacher caught him with his school uniform not worn appropriately. Doing his job like he usually would, the teacher loudly asked the child to adjust his uniform properly, to which the child ignored him because this teenager also has a certain dislike toward this particular teacher. The teacher raised his voice louder to get the teen to comply. This time, the child defiantly shouted, "Why should I?" This made the teacher fuming mad, and it escalated quickly toward a threat made against the teacher.

The child is required to apologize immediately for being disrespectful. Otherwise, he would be given detention. The child angrily apologizes. Did the teacher "win"? Probably! He probably did by virtue of his positional authority over the child — being the teacher in charge of disciplinary matters in the school. However, the teacher would have lost the relational authority over the child right there. The possibility of the teacher being able to sit the child down and teach him a lesson on, say, respect, even to relate an inspirational story about respect, is near zero. The child would probably "switch off" and not listen.

As teachers and especially parents, we never want to be in this situation. We want our teenagers to always have their doors open to us so that we can guide and teach them, even when they are upset or angry. This is especially critical if the child has no one to turn to, or may be in some difficult situation. Like in the same example above, the disciplinary teacher did not know something happened earlier that day to the child. The child was already angry, and the teacher experienced a retaliation from the child with "Why should I?"

If I were to continue with the same level of emotions as the teacher did, I would have lost an opportunity to find out what happened to the child, and the opportunity to provide the necessary support and understanding the child may need then. I would definitely require the child to adhere to proper school decorum at some point, but the question is whether it should be at that moment in time.

One may argue that it may not necessarily be a near impossible task to reach out to the child again, which is a valid argument. However, the point is about needing to effectively engage the child, and convey the message or lesson to the child with the intent to do so **not** just at that moment, but in the next few weeks, months, and years. Hence, it is not about who wins or loses either. The supposed "parenting war" with adolescents is theoretically for a window of ten years. If you want to parent well, and develop a trusting developmental relationship with your child for the many years to come, it should not matter if you "win or lose" some battles in the short term. It is the "war" that we want to win; it is the long-term relationship we want to have with our child that is more important.

Your child needs you — the parent! Every child needs their parent, regardless of whether they express it or not. It is extremely hard for the child to appreciate this fact. Yet, in families with deep positive relationships between parents and teen, when the child goes through a difficult time, the child would often think about their parents! We cannot say the same for dysfunctional families. All teens are going through a tumultuous phase of their lives. Hence, achieving strong relational authority over them is far more desirable then achieving strong positional authority over them — the short-term wins. The latter is counterproductive and all efforts to build that developmental relationship with the child would be futile when there is no relational authority.

Youth Engagement Matrix

Youth Emotional Dispositions	Limbic Strategies	Prefrontal Strategies
Positive Emotions	✓ Engage	✓ Engage
Negative Emotions	✓ Engage (Positively)	✗ Do not engage

In subsequent chapters, I will be providing this matrix as a guide to assist parents in deciding if they want to engage their teenager better. It would serve as a very useful guide to help you regulate your efforts in a more sustainable way toward building a strong relational authority with the adolescents, even toward building that desired developmental relationship with your child.

SUMMARY

1. The hallmark of adolescence is marked by emotional changes and reliance, observed by several key changes in youth:
   a. Intense and unpredictable emotional phases.

b. Increased emotional reactivity.
   c. Gradual awareness and identification of emotions.
   d. Increased self-consciousness and social comparison of physical appearance.
   e. Poor consequential thinking and irrational decision-making.
2. Parents and their youth often experience a mismatch in expectations — parents expect youth to engage in productive and positive behavior, while youth are naturally driven toward unproductive and gratifying behavior. This mismatch can be divisive and relationally harmful if parents are adamant on their choices.
3. Youth often exhibit three common behaviors:
   a. A constant need to prove themselves as grown-up, along with assuming that they understand the reason of things.
   b. A strong imagination and tendency to experience *personal fable*.
   c. A self-centered perspective that assumes the world is watching them.
4. Although youth are naturally limbic responders, parents can help them develop prefrontal thought processes with empathetic support and processing of their limbic tendencies.
5. Parents should strive to develop strong relational authority, as opposed to using positional authority with their youth.

Chapter 7

Mind of Dopamine

An adolescent's mind is developing. It is growing in size and number of neuro-connections every day with numerous amounts of life events and learning. We need to find ways of making the mind of adolescents more resilient and flexible. The changes the mind goes through in the adolescence period remain with the person as his personality features in the form of multiple feelings and logical reasons.

Though the part of the brain that has logic and reasoning develops later toward the end of the adolescence period, there is sufficient development throughout the teenage years to count on. These qualities really need to stay to help the teens navigate the world in their own person. These essential qualities have potential power. And, this power resides within the child, accompanied by all his efforts and actions. With this power, the young person can choose to live a meaningful life.

The ability to see and realize the qualities within the young person and make them strong enough to stay powerful throughout life is their mental abilities. The power is really the internal strength that can only be moved by the child; parents and adults can help to nudge the child to action, but ultimately the power to act and overcome lies in the child. So, the ability to truly know and understand the mind as its whole function is our focus now in this part of the book.

We need three basic skills to know our mind and discover its abilities:

1. **Insight:** It is a sensory skill which gives us a clear vision of our inner mental approach, for example, who we have been throughout the past years and what we are visualizing ourselves to become in the future. With this skill, we are able to connect our past with the present and also to our future. So, we know clearly who we are.

2. **Empathy:** This is a sensory skill through which we know the inner mental approach of another person. This skill enables us to see things from the perspective of the other person. In other words, we are able to walk in another person's shoes and know how things are. It is key to social intelligence. With the help of this skill, we know the intentions of other persons and we are able to connect with them in a more mutually satisfying manner.

3. **Integration:** This mental ability helps us to link the different parts of something and make it into a whole complete structure. This skill is advanced. It enables us to connect the different parts of something. Hence, we are able to promote sympathetic connections while we communicate. With this skill, we are able to connect the different parts of our memories and understand our own life story. At the same time, we are able to form a link between our brain and body. This leads to better functioning and healthy living.

These three skills help us live a healthy life, have healthy relationships, and have healthy minds.

Let me explain further how these three skills of knowing our minds better can help us. Think of a hot day. What would you usually like to do? You may think of multiple options like going skateboarding or being by the pool or eating ice cream. Of course, we love to go to the pool and enjoy a splashing cool time. So, this is a fun choice and very suitable on a hot day. However, if we miss skateboarding, we may miss the upcoming competition with the other guys. Staying out of practice is bad because we will not improve.

So, our mind quickly takes a deep look inside it and connects the things to make a link between our desires and our successes, between the present and our future. Hence, we quickly reach the conclusion that we need to practice skateboarding in order to win the competition. It is a brighter option for our future.

But, studies and our earlier discussion in this book reveals that adolescents will naturally fail to have these insights and integration. They rather follow short-term desires and do what they want at the moment. Pursuing long-term goals is often absent from their mind. The weak connections and the absence of insight into their inner mind make them fail to choose the better option for their present and future.

The inability of adolescents to think with more insight and integration is natural. In fact, they are known for their impulsive behavior. So, they do several things without thinking much about them in the present or the consequences in the future. This is called **impulsivity**.

Doing things without going deep inside the mind and viewing consequences of an action like advantages or disadvantages can be of much good for adolescents. They are still young and need a lot of new experiences to learn from. Moreover, they are more tempted to do exciting tasks rather than indulging in boring options. For learning new things and earning good experiences, they really need to indulge in several different things that they impulsively do.

There is more growth of **dopamine receptors** during the teen years of life. This enhanced supply of dopamine during the adolescence period provides a rush of high emotions like immense pleasure and excitement. This dopamine release gives adolescents a strong sense of liveliness while they engage in and live life.

Daniel Siegel, Clinical Professor of Psychiatry at the University of California, Los Angeles, School of Medicine, and the author of the book *Brainstorm: The Power and Purpose of the Teenage Brain*, highlighted that dopamine can also lead adolescents to focus solely on the positive rewards they are sure are in store for them, while failing to notice or give value to the potential risks and downsides.

Siegel also mentioned that the brain's increased drive for reward in adolescents manifests in the teenagers' lives in three important ways:

(i) **Increased impulsiveness:** This is where behaviors occur without thoughtful reflection. In other words, impulse inspires action without any pause. Pausing enables us to think about other options beyond the immediate dopamine-driven impulse pounding in our minds. Telling that impulse to chill out takes time and energy, so it is easier just not to do it. This said, with the drive for reward stronger and more pressing than ever when we are teens, taking the time needed for processing — for reflection and self-awareness — becomes very important. If any notion turns immediately into action without reflection, we are living our lives all gas pedal and no brakes.

(ii) **Susceptibility to addiction:** All behaviors and substances that are addictive involve the release of dopamine. As teens, not only are we more likely to experiment with new experiences but we are also more prone to respond with a robust dopamine release that for some can become part of an addictive cycle. A drug, alcohol, for example, can lead to release of dopamine, and we may feel compelled to ingest beer, wine, or hard liquor. When the alcohol wears off, our dopamine plummets. We then are driven to use more of the substance that spiked our dopamine circuits.

(iii) **Hyperrationality:** This is how we think in literal, concrete terms. We examine just the facts of a situation and do not see the big picture; we miss the setting or context in which those facts occur. This is not a lack of thought or reflection as happens with impulsivity, and it is not a matter of merely being addicted to a particular behavior or something we are ingesting. With such literal thinking, as adolescents, we can place more weight on the calculated benefits of an action than on the potential risks of that action. Studies reveal that as teens, we are often fully aware of risks, and even at times overestimate the chance of something bad happening; we simply put more weight on the exciting potential benefits of our actions.

Research suggests that risky behaviors in adolescence have less to do with hormonal imbalances than with changes in our brain's dopamine reward system combined with the cortical architecture that supports hyperrational decision-making — creating the positive bias that is dominant during the teenage years.

All these can be extremely stressful for adolescents and the adults who care for them. However, it is not all doom and gloom; Siegel mentioned that such increased drive for reward in adolescents can be put on hold if certain fibers in the higher part of the brain work to create a mental space between impulse and action. This is where parents, the adults, play an important role in using the strategies proposed throughout the book to facilitate and assist the young person in making limbic–frontal neuro-connections, so that the mental space between impulse and action, specifically, the limbic system and prefrontal cortex, is filled with the fibers necessary to control the impulsivities.

It is during this adolescence period that these regulatory fibers begin to grow and strengthen, to counteract the revved up "go" of the dopamine reward system. According to Siegel, this is sometimes called "cognitive control" and it is important for the minimizing of danger and the reducing of risks as adolescents grow and develop.

There are essential tools for training and guiding adolescents to grow up into better thinking and better behaving adults. If these tools are properly used to help the cognitive development of kids, we can be assured that our teens will grow into adults who are highly skillful, intelligent, and understanding. We propose five skills in the next chapter.

SUMMARY

1. Insight, empathy, and integration are the three essential mental skills to develop the youth's lives, relationships, and minds in a healthy manner.
2. Youth experience an enhanced growth of dopamine receptors, which provides them with a rush of high emotions like pleasure and excitement. This often leads to increased impulsiveness, susceptibility to addiction, and hyperrationality.
3. Parents can facilitate the development of cognitive control in the youth, to help counteract their increased impulsivity.

Chapter 8

Five Cognitive Controls

As mentioned in the previous chapter, we are going to discuss and propose some essential tools to train and guide adolescents. We will also introduce the use of the Youth Engagement Matrix and the Developmental Relationship Elements (DREs) Targeting Checklist.

The suggested tools or approaches may be used to target some of the developmental relationship elements. We encourage some intentional or purposeful engagement with your teens, bearing in mind that they are ultimately "limbic responders."

Therefore, when we indicate on the Youth Engagement Matrix for you to engage, you may do so discerningly. We highlighted earlier that parents know their kids the best. While one strategy that is used with one child works, this does not mean it will work with another child. Each child is different in every aspect of their growth and development.

TOOL # 1 — COGNITIVE CONTROL

Cognitive control is one part of attention training. Attention training aims to let teens practice so as to keep their minds on one point of focus. The moment their minds wander off, bring their attention back to that point. Neuroscientists find that the natural outcome of this practice makes the adolescents' brain circuitries stronger. As a result of that, the brain can harness the negative emotions and impulsive behaviors whenever the need arises, or at will.

Cognitive development and control are critical throughout the teen years. So, we learn here to understand the development of cognitive control with the development of the brain. Children continue to learn throughout their childhood and adolescence to control their actions to display better mental performance and to achieve future goals. The changes continue to happen in the cognitive system. In fact, these are functional and structural changes and we can help the adolescents' brain work out fully and develop in the right direction and at the right speed. Also, we aim to enable teens to learn from their experiences and have the maximum opportunity to execute behaviors that are positive, productive, and purposeful.

We want to help the teens engage the two hemispheres of the cerebrum and the two hemispheres of the cerebellum. The key point here is that this engagement is very much needed in real life. The activities of everyday life and engagements in a number of learning programs, sports, and social events all help teens learn and improve cognitive control.

Neuroscientists have generally suggested five exercises that can improve cognitive control in adolescents.

Brain Gyms

There are several brain-teasing and training games like puzzles, quizzes, mazes, and thought-provoking questions specially designed to activate brain abilities. These quizzes and puzzles improve cognitive control in teens. Engagement in such games regularly sharpens a teen's brain, especially when it is in the developing stage.

Social Connections

It is great to have social connections. In the company of other adolescents, teens feel excited, motivated, and flexible. But, teens do not know how to choose their social circle, and we cannot impose on them a certain social connection to keep them safe from bad company.

We need to be indirect in our efforts with them because teens do not like to be controlled and dislike being told what to do and what not to do. Our behaviors with the teens and the type of life we live with them shape up their choices.

Youth Engagement Matrix

Youth Emotional Dispositions	Limbic Strategies	Prefrontal Strategies
Positive Emotions	✓ Engage	
Negative Emotions	✓ Engage (Positively)	

For example, a father who plays music at home among his family induces good family emotions in the heart of his children.

From a very young age, they learn positivity and amicability. Hence, it automatically shapes up their choice of friends

Another father who plays soccer with his kids from a very young age encourages them to be in a soccer team, not a gang. Yet another father who frequently invites his friends' families over and lets his kids mingle with his friends' kids gives them the opportunity to develop healthy social bonds.

Creativity and Innovation

Creative activities, crafts, and arts help the teens develop their cognitive powers very fast as well as their cognitive control. Rex LaMore, Director of Michigan State University's Center for Community and Economic Development, reported that engaging in arts and crafts leads to immense mental strength in the field of innovation, creative ideas, and patents. Researchers at the Center discovered that successful business owners were exposed to arts and crafts as children eight times more than the normal public. The most interesting finding was the importance of sustained participation in those activities.

LaMore highlighted that "if you started as a young child and continued in your adult years, you are more likely to be an inventor as measured by the number of patents generated, businesses formed, or articles published." And this is really something that we should all note.

Gottfried Schlaug, a medical doctor, researcher, an expert on music, neuroimaging, and brain plasticity from Harvard Medical School, echoed that "these insights suggest potential new roles for musical training including fostering plasticity in the brain, and have strong implications for using musical training as a tool in education, and for treating a range of learning disabilities."

DRE
Targeting Checklist

Developmental Relationship Elements	Check
V VOICE	
O SHOW	
I INSPIRE	✓
C CHALLENGE	✓
E ENCOURAGE	✓

New Experiences

Often parents are reluctant to allow their teens to be involved in new experiences. For example, a camping program at the foothills is often looked at with extreme caution. In another case, when a teen is interested in learning a new skill, parents find it quite demanding and they do not allow their teen to waste his time and effort in it, for example, pottery or woodwork.

Researchers have a very different opinion on these. They do not find any brain development in simple activities and missions. They say that in order to give the teens' brain a push to learn and manage control, they should be allowed to go out. They must be involved in doing something unfamiliar and, preferably, mentally challenging. Let them come out of their comfort zone and experience different aspects of outside life.

Physical Activity

It is a known fact now that physical activity improves brain's function. There are several studies at numerous universities that prove this fact. There are many pieces of evidence on the effects of physical activity on fast cognitive development.

Certain hormones improve from exercise and physical activities; these hormones enhance the brain's ability to think, perform, and control. During exercise, certain molecules are released that brighten the cognitive function and enhance memory as well. All these positive effects of exercise create a strong improvement program for the cognitive function. Hence, encouraging teens to get involved in physical exercise as much as possible is highly recommended. Irisin is a special molecule in the brain which develops through a chain reaction during endurance exercises. It has neuroprotective effects which are all about learning and memory.

TOOL # 2 — INNER WORLD

In order to enable adolescents to develop their brain better, we need another essential tool called "inner world." This means to look at your inner life — our own mind's life. Why is this important? Spending some time with a focus on what is going on inside our own brains helps our brains maintain strong and healthy circuits. This is necessary for integration in our practical lives and thinking. Focusing on our outside world is not enough. We need our mind to have an insight into its own inner world. This creates integration in our lives and improves our empathy.

DRE
Targeting Checklist

Developmental Relationship Elements	Check
V VOICE	
O SHOW	
I INSPIRE	✓
C CHALLENGE	
E ENCOURAGE	✓

Making it a habit to look deep inside our own brains is helpful because it helps exercise our own brain circuits to integrate our brain functions and improve our life. There is one method of inner world focus. Start developing mindful awareness. It is a way of training which enables us to stay present with recent happenings. So, instead of accepting life the way it is, we focus on how we expect it to be.

Focusing the mind on its inner world is called "meditation," and studies reveal how mindfulness meditation supports healthier functions in the body and in the mind. Because of the immense benefits of meditation, we need to implant in the minds of our adolescents the habit of mindfulness meditation. This helps us be present in our lives. This habit sometimes develops in people automatically, but others need to develop it. Being present in life increases the level of the enzyme telomerase. These enzymes are very important in our long living process. This enzyme repairs the life-preserving ends of our chromosomes which are called telomere caps. The everyday stress of life and the aging process whittles these enzymes. But, we are able to build more telomerase which can further help us live longer and healthier. Mindfulness training helps the brain learn to be present for its inner world. This increases immunity and the level of telomerase.

This is an amazing thing that we can help our adolescents grow with. The mind's focus on the inner side can change molecules in our body which makes us healthier and live longer. The same habit of being present in our inner side keeps us aware of our emotions. Hence, we can harness our emotions for our benefit and not leave them working against us. The ability to focus on our tasks and the interest in learning increase. The benefits of meditation continue to come to light with more research, and the studies show that the ability of a person to approach life increases and he does not withdraw from any challenge he faces. It is a way to live our lives with meaningfulness.

Let us make it simpler and more practical for you to understand:

You may have asked your teen a question some time in his life or many times and he would have replied, "I do not know."

This is true; teens do not have the full impulse control to understand the reasons behind things. During adolescence, the frontal lobe of the brain is still in the developing stage and cannot always communicate well with the amygdala, which is responsible for a direct response to trigger quite instinctively. So, the connections between the frontal lobe and amygdala are not strong. We know that with age they will become strong, but why not help them get stronger faster through meditation? The brain benefits immensely from meditation and responds faster to the triggers with connections between the amygdala and the frontal lobe. This is especially helpful for those teens who suffer from more anxiety and clumsy behavior.

There are several sets of meditation suggested by the experts and for different durations. If you choose any of those sets, you can help your brain immensely. Once the brain is triggered with the help of meditation to strengthen links between the frontal lobe and the amygdala, it will continue getting stronger with each session of meditation. The advantages of meditation are easing of stress and anxiety, better focus, strong imagination, etc.

Tyler Jacobson, a journalist and frequent writer for Parenting Blogs, wrote in his article "Teenagers Can Benefit from Meditation" at PsychCentral, "clearing the mind and reducing stress is important, but what real importance does meditation have in today's scientifically-driven society? A lot, as it turns out. Studies show that over time, meditation increases the gray matter density in your brain, helping with memory, empathy, and decision-making. Meditation also dismantles the connections between the medial prefrontal cortex, responsible for your perspective of self, and the amygdala, which is where fear comes from. The brain then reconnects the amygdala to the lateral prefrontal cortex, which is what allows you to see the situation from a rational standpoint. Over time, when your teen becomes afraid or stressed, they stop assuming it's because of them and instead can see situations more clearly."

Jacobson further highlighted that "along with the hard science of meditation, there are also numerous emotional benefits. All of the stress our teens undergo is not a light strain. It takes energy and thought to constantly concern themselves with all of their past mistakes and worries for the future. It does not exactly leave space for being aware of the now. By helping our teens learn to stop, clear the mind, and just look at things as they are, we are not only helping to unload a lot of constant mental weight, but also better management of their emotions. When it comes to depression, teens' ability to observe their own thoughts without judgment and recognize emotional triggers gives them more self-understanding. It can help lessen rumination and keep them from getting caught up in a downward spiral."

Therefore, the brain goes through significant changes during meditation. It discards connections that it does not need anymore. It also creates more new connections which give a person a clearer perspective of things. Basically, during adolescence, the brain is developing connections, and when this process is helped by meditation, the development increases and with time, these connections become stronger. Teens develop an ability to clear their minds and calm down their emotions. When they need to deliver a speech or give a test, the practice of meditation becomes helpful.

When life moves on with the teens and they are practicing meditation, they will understand their surroundings better and have a clearer image of the world around them. Their own toxic thoughts would not distort reality for them. Moreover, they will make connections and judge situations based on the data they observe and have a stronger sense of empathy for others. Here, a sense of strong confidence calmly sets in alone with the feeling of being in control of their lives and actions.

Dan Siegel has designed a meditation program for teens in his book *Brainstorm*. The following is a practical and helpful guide:

Guidance

The first time you do this, get started with a focus on the visible outside world. With your eyes open, let your attention focus on the middle of the room. Now send your attention to the far wall or ceiling. Now direct your visual attention to the middle of the room again. And now bring your attention to about book reading distance, as if you have a book or magazine in your hands. Notice how you can direct the focus of attention.

For this practice, let the sensation of the breath be the object of attention. Let's begin at the level of the nostrils with the subtle sensation of the air coming in and going out. Ride the wave of the breath, in and out, and just sense that sensation. Now notice how you can direct attention from the nostrils to the chest. Let the sensation of the chest rising and falling fill awareness. Up and down, simply ride the wave of the breath in and out.

Now redirect attention to the abdomen. If you are new to this abdominal breathing, you can place a hand on the belly and simply notice how the abdomen moves out when air fills the lungs, and the abdomen moves in when air escapes the lungs.

Simply ride the wave of the breath by focusing attention on the sensation of the breath wherever it feels most natural. It may be the abdomen moving in and out, the chest rising and falling, or the air at the nostrils. Or it may simply be the whole body breathing. Just let the sensation of the breath fill awareness wherever you feel it most readily. As you ride the wave of the breath, in and out, let's take a few moments to focus on an ancient story that's been passed down through the generations.

The Story

The story goes like this. The mind is like the ocean. And deep beneath the surface of the ocean, it is calm and clear. From this place of clarity beneath the surface, it is possible to just look up and notice whatever conditions are at the surface.

It may be flat, or choppy with waves, or there may even be a full storm, but no matter the conditions, deep beneath the surface it remains calm and clear. The mind is like the ocean. And just sensing the breath brings you beneath the surface of the mind. From this deep place in the mind, it is possible to notice whatever surface activity is happening in the mind, such as feelings or thoughts, memories, or ideas.

From this deep place beneath the surface of the mind, it is calm and clear. And just sensing the breath brings you to this mind, it is calm and clear. And just sensing the breath brings you to this place of clarity and tranquility. Now let's return to a focus of attention on the sensation of the breath wherever you feel it most readily.

Just ride the wave of the breath, in and out. For this basic mindfulness of the breath practice, we'll take time-in to simply let the sensation of the breath fill awareness. When something distracts attention away from the breath and you've come to notice that awareness is no longer filled with the sensation of the breath, just notice the distraction and then let it go, returning the focus of attention to the breath and filling awareness with the sensation of the breath.

Personal Journey

We will practice this mindfulness of the breath now for a few minutes. (If you have a timer, you can set it to whatever duration you like, five minutes, a dozen, twenty.) As you experience the practice, you may find your attention goes to something other than the breath. For some, naming the distraction helps to let it go. For others, such naming is itself a distraction. If you choose to give this a try, it is often helpful to give the distraction the same general name as the kind of distraction that took your attention away.

So if the memory of being at the beach distracts your attention, then you can simply say quietly in your mind, "Remembering, remembering, remembering," and let the memory go. For some, this can be helpful to strengthen their ability to release a distraction and return the focus of attention to the breath. For others, it is not helpful and may even be distracting. Find what works for you.

Remember, in addition to the task of simply focusing on the breath, it is recommended that you consider regarding yourself with kindness as you go through this practice. Everyone's mind wanders at times, and that is just what it means to be human.

In fact, part of the strengthening aspect of this practice comes from the redirecting of attention, which is like contracting a muscle. The unintentional distractions are like relaxing a muscle, the refocusing on the breath is the tightening of the muscle. Focus, distraction, refocus, distraction, refocus again.

That is how we work out our minds with this time-in practice. This time-in can be new to many, focusing on the internal sensations of our mental lives. If you find yourself getting sleepy, you can always open your eyes a bit if they are closed. And if that doesn't help to energize the mind, you can try this exercise standing up. Same practice, exercise standing up. Same practice, only now you are vertical.

Let's give this a try. After a designated period of time, when you are ready, you can take a more intentional and perhaps deeper breath and let your eyes come open if they are shut, and we'll bring this time-in breath awareness practice to a close.

How was that for you? If you are new to this, welcome! As we said, this may be simple, but it is not easy for most of us. The mind does get distracted easily, and that is just part of the reality of having a human mind. To carry out this practice, we train our minds to be present. With repeated practice, this mind-training exercise has been shown to grow important parts of the brain that are connected not only with attention but with emotion and empathy as well. These are integrative circuits, and so this basic mindfulness of the breath practice helps integrate the brain. It is a form of brain health, a way of creating mental resilience and well-being.

TOOL # 3 — OBSERVATION

Children have the power of observation. From the start of their lives, they begin observing their surroundings, parents, family members, and the outside world. They grow up with a lot of new things in their minds that they have learned through observation. They learn language, behavior, and reactions through observation. This is all natural and the process goes on with them throughout their childhood until they enter their teens.

After the start of the teen years of life, observation becomes a strong tool for learning. Teens with stronger observational power pass in tests and win competitions of different sorts. But, the question is if all teens have the ability to employ their observational power positively. Some teens do not use observation as a learning tool in their everyday life, while some other teens learn negative things faster through observation like the violence that they watch in video games and TV series.

Experts agree that observation is a powerful tool for learning.

Psychologist Albert Bandura has noted in his research that the most obvious way to learn is observation. Along with others researchers, he has demonstrated that humans are naturally more likely to engage in observational learning.

We can use this theory for good application with adolescents who are in the stage of learning and developing behavior. Also, their minds are developing and any practice can help build better connections.

According to Bandura, we are more likely to imitate the following:

(i) People we perceive as warm and nurturing,
(ii) People who receive rewards for their behavior,

(iii) When you have been rewarded for imitating the behavior in the past,
(iv) When we lack confidence in our own knowledge or abilities,
(v) People who are in an authoritative position in our lives,
(vi) People who are similar to us in age, sex, and interests,
(vii) People who we admire or who are of a higher social status,
(viii) When the situation is confusing, ambiguous, or unfamiliar.

Kendra Cherry, author of *The Everything Psychology Book* and educator with over a decade of experience helping students make sense of psychology, said that "observational learning can be a powerful learning tool. When we think about the concept of learning, we often talk about direct instruction or methods that rely on reinforcement and punishment. But a great deal of learning takes place much more subtly and relies on watching the people around us and modeling their actions. This learning method can be applied in a wide range of settings including job training, education, counseling, and psychotherapy."

When we talk about observation, we emphasize the benefits of observation on the adolescent learning process. Observation helps the teens learn more and faster. But, leaving them to their own devices to increase observation is not sufficient to build a strong ability to observe. We need to build an unbreakable habit of observation in our teens throughout their teen years. This is a fertile learning period when everything you learn is saved in your memory. A person needs observational powers throughout his life, when he is a student, an employee, a family member, a citizen, etc. There are a number of issues in a teen's thinking process, judgment, learning, and understanding, which are a result of poor observation.

Youth Engagement Matrix

Youth Emotional Dispositions	Limbic Strategies	Prefrontal Strategies
Positive Emotions	✓ Engage	
Negative Emotions	✓ Engage (Positively)	

When we strengthen the observation power in teens through different sorts of exercises and quizzes at school, we encourage them to use this observational power in order to be successful. Many students show a lack of interest in and a lack of attention for their lessons. Teachers find them not focusing on the explanations they deliver in regard to the studies. Often, the students fall asleep during the class. This is just one negative impact of weak observation. There are several more examples in the real life of teens where the lack of observation or misuse of observation is clearly present.

By incorporating different types of quizzes, puzzles, and questions about real-life incidents in the daily activities at school, we can encourage the students to observe their surroundings, the behavior of people, natural events, and least obvious incidents. Once the teens develop a habit of observation, they do not forget it or ignore it. In fact, it is an interesting process and an observer earns the benefits of observation most of the times. This is the reason why teens easily accept the suggestion to observe everything in the environment.

At home, parents can indirectly encourage teens to observe things around them, for example, giving them tasks that need a lot of observation. These tasks should be interesting like observing things around the room and finding some things which need to be packed away due to not being in use, for example. Gardening, shopping, going for a stroll outdoors, and many other practical tasks can be a great opportunity to improve observation.

DRE
Targeting Checklist

Developmental Relationship Elements	Check
V VOICE	
O SHOW	
I INSPIRE	✓
C CHALLENGE	
E ENCOURAGE	✓

Learning anything in life based on observation is a powerful learning method that never fails. Often, learning is based on what is obvious and clear, but learning through things which are hidden and can be understood only by observation is a strong learning method that always helps a person learn new methods in life.

Parents can encourage their teens to interact with nature at all times for different time spans, for example, going out in the rain with an umbrella, working in the garden after dawn, picking cherries from the trees in the evening, and going for a walk along a river and feeding the ducks.

Engaging in observational activities strengthens the brain to add powerful connections within itself. New learning strikes the brain to work with more awareness. This is thrilling most of the times and when teens learn to do observation frequently, they tend to learn things fast and develop a strong base of experience.

For many, the daily incidents are nothing but just happenings not worthy of any attention. But, this is not the case. Everything has some significance and deserves our observation of its intricate sides. A child looking lost in a crowd, a girl sitting alone on a bench in the park, two young kids making fun of one another, a bird building a nest on a tree, and many other little incidents are worth observation. In fact, each of these happenings has something to teach us.

TOOL # 4 — LET THEM TALK

Do you know that most of the parents love to lecture their teens and "advice" them? They do not bother to listen to their kids and find out what is in their hearts and minds. Most of the times, they find it their duty to say something or pass comments on the actions, trends, habits, behavior, and looks of people. The thought that teens are nothing but "raging hormones" and they are illogical is the biggest reason why the parents do not give a chance to their teens to talk and, hence, do not bother to listen to them.

DRE

Targeting Checklist

Developmental Relationship Elements	Check
V VOICE	✓
O SHOW	✓
I INSPIRE	
C CHALLENGE	
E ENCOURAGE	✓

As a matter of fact, teens have a lot on their minds to talk about and share especially with a loved one. They do not feel comfortable around unfriendly behavior and keep mum most of the times even if something is bothering them.

Encouraging teens to talk by striking a conversation around anything important in their lives is a great way to build the confidence of your child. For example, your daughter loves photography. Talk with her about her area of interest. But, it should not be you who does most of the talking. You strike ideas and let her talk. You can ask questions during her talk, but give her maximum time to speak. Show interest and listen.

In fact, it is difficult to listen! You want to shift your mindset from thinking ahead for them and providing information, to one that is curiously listening. The process of listening to your teens is not just listening. It is time to process what they say. You gather their thoughts and observations in your mind and process them for the good of the whole family. You need to know what your teen is thinking and where his interests are taking him. Most of the times, the teens are not coherent. They have not yet built the art of presenting their thoughts. Actually, they are still developing the skill of talking, understanding, and reasoning. You are there to help them talk so that they practice saying it. You need to give them a chance to talk and be listened to so that they feel confident and have the satisfaction of a parent listening to them.

It is when parents actually refuse to listen that they can be silently abusive. They won't take the time. They won't devote their attention. They won't show the interest. "You never listen to me!" complains the teenager, acting hurt because the message he takes to heart may be "I'm not worth listening to!"

That's one important point for parents to remember: listening affirms that the speaker has something worthwhile to say. Not listening denies or dismisses that value.

The second point is that listening is an investment the parent needs to make. Make no investment in listening and there may be no listening or speaking up in return. "Why should I listen or talk to you when you never listen to me!" Listening enables communication. Not listening shuts down both aspects of communication.

However, parents need to understand that the teenager's readiness to talk in a seriously self-disclosing way depends on happenstance, emotion, and mood coming into some mysterious internal alignment that sets the stage for momentary openness to occur — all factors that she does not usually control. "I don't feel like talking now" is often not a lame excuse, but a psychologically valid explanation.

TOOL # 5 — THINKING SKILLS

Youth Engagement Matrix

Youth Emotional Dispositions	Limbic Strategies	Prefrontal Strategies
Positive Emotions		✓ Engage
Negative Emotions		✗ Do Not Engage

The prefrontal cortex (PFC) is still under development. This part of the brain is mainly responsible for controlling impulses, taking decisions, having logical reasons for anything, etc. One thing we are sure about is that the PFC is busy in the teen years of life in wiring the basic skills for critical thinking. Naturally, the PFC is connected to other parts of the brain. Hence, it receives input from each part and its job is to connect the information exactly as you connect the dots to make a picture. The job of the PFC is complex. It is developing and improving its skills of analyzing cause and effect, foreseeing future consequences, and relating objects, principles, and concepts. It is also nurturing creativity, insight, empathy, reasoning, esthetic judgment, and caring. Teens start learning to make rational decisions, knitting plans, setting goals, getting organized, and managing thoughts for various tasks.

This age is the right time for them to get prepared for the life-long brain performance that will determine their future, career, success, and even the level of their humanity. Each time a teen learns critical thinking and tries to put it into practice, he helps his brain reinforce the capacity for further critical thinking. Most probably, each time it gets better and stronger.

Why do people grow up differently? One reason is that their critical thinking skills are not equally developed. Some people have a good foundation for critical thinking, while others do not. They think differently. They act differently and end up yielding benefits differently.

Here is an example:

Ben is writing an application for a job vacancy. He knows his skills, but he wants to write them in an eye-catching manner. At the same time, he is thinking about choosing only those skills which are highly related to this job and describing them in an impressive manner, keeping in mind the perspective of his employer.

This is Ben's critical thinking moment.

Bill is also writing an application for a job interview. He quickly writes down his skills and describes his abilities for the available job and ends his application.

Bill did not flex his brain to think critically about writing the job application.

The end result was Ben selected for the job and Bill rejected!

This is just one example of how critical thinking makes people part ways from their peers and one either proves to be brilliantly successful or ends up failing at demanding and complicated tasks.

Training teenagers on critical thinking starts from a very young age; some experts encourage the parents to start training young kids at age 7 or 8 to think critically on a small scale. This is a good practice especially when the parents have a clear idea or plan about how they will take this critical thinking to higher levels. But, you can start it after your kid hits his teens if you did not have a clear idea of it before.

Parents need to care about the critical thinking ability of their teens. After becoming full adults, the ability to act right and with a powerful force depends on how much an adult is able to exercise his critical thinking. That is why you see that some adults have enough brain power to occupy high-profile jobs and progress, while some others simply cannot.

It is good practice to start critical thinking at an early stage because it takes time for a teen to incorporate the skills fully in his thinking. Often, he fails to get a hang of the process. Hence, several mistakes can happen from your child. This should not have a negative impact on you. A child may fail several times fully or partially. This is natural. What you can do to keep him going willingly is to keep calm and positive. Do not show that you are disappointed, tired of him, or just not able to maintain his training on critical thinking.

Will the child accept to start thinking critically?

From the child's perspective, it is hard to cope with the training because their brain is still at the development stage, especially the PFC. Moreover, the idea is new for her and she cannot visualize the importance of critical thinking for her future. She tries to think critically as much as she can. Often, the parents think she is not doing her best or she is not trying to understand. This is not the case with teens. They simply need revised and repeated sessions of training so that it becomes smooth for them to follow the process.

So, developing critical thinking from scratch can take time, effort, and much patience. It may take all the adolescence of the kids for the parents to build critical thinking in the minds of their teens. But, it is worth the effort. In fact, brain development is a slow, silent, and invisible process and it reaches its final stage without anyone realizing it. Once a person becomes an adult, it is almost impossible to train him on critical thinking. In the next chapter, we shall discuss the five best ways for developing critical thinking skills in teens.

SUMMARY

There are five essential tools that parents can use to train their youth.

1. Developing cognitive control through five exercises:
   a. Brain gyms.

b. Social connections.
   c. Creative activities.
   d. New experiences.
   e. Physical activities.
2. Achieving mindful awareness of their inner world through developing the habit of meditation.
3. Sharpening their observational learning by teaching them to focus on subtle, intricate details.
4. Developing conversational confidence and coherent thought processes by letting them speak more and using prompting questions.
5. Developing critical thinking through constant engagement in analytical and consequential thinking.

Chapter 9
Developing High-Level Thinking

Critical thinking is an extremely high-level thinking for adolescents. For them to develop this skill, it takes time and they require the help and support of the adults. This high-level thinking needs to start from scratch and will take time, effort, and much patience. The journey may be a really rough one, but very often it is also a worthwhile and meaningful one. When youth start to take meaningful and responsible decisions, they thrive and excel. That moment for parents is priceless!

Youth Engagement Matrix

Youth Emotional Dispositions	Limbic Strategies	Prefrontal Strategies
Positive Emotions		✓ Engage
Negative Emotions		✗ Do Not Engage

During the process, all the effort can be perceived to not pay off very much, as the brain develops in a slow, quiet, and invisible manner. However, science and neuroimaging have shown us repeatedly that the brain does reach its final stages of development. Once the brain is fully developed, it is very challenging to train the teenager to adopt this high-level thinking.

So, here are five powerful ways to help adolescents develop critical thinking.

ASSIGN CHALLENGING TASKS

DRE

Targeting Checklist

Developmental Relationship Elements	Check
V VOICE	
O SHOW	
I INSPIRE	✓
C CHALLENGE	✓
E ENCOURAGE	✓

Challenges and difficult-to-solve problems give the brain a good exercise. Most often, teens do not encounter challenges in their daily life. Mostly, it is a routine life of going to school and spending weekends with friends or family. To help the brain of your teen to start thinking critically and using his prefrontal cortex (PFC), you need to find some good challenging tasks in practical life.

There are several examples of doing something challenging within a certain time frame, money limit, and study level, and home tasks like cooking, gardening, decorating the home for festivities, decluttering the storeroom, repairing or renewing old furniture, painting the home, and cleaning windows are good examples.

You can give your child some cash and ask him to buy a healthy and nutritious meal for two. Now, managing to get what is healthy, nutritious, and filling at the same time needs some thinking and calculation. This is good practice for the child's brain to come up with a solution that meets the requirements.

Another example is to give your teen any home task to complete within a certain time frame. To make it more friendly and interesting, you can also join him, and either you do the same work side by side or choose another task at home and get involved in it keenly to set a practical example for the youth to work and complete tasks assigned to them.

There come several levels in each task, which need some critical thinking. Often, there are two or more ways to choose from and it needs some thinking to choose one and not the other. So, let there be one challenging task ready for your kid every short period of time. You will see that he comes up with questions sometimes and at other times he happily narrates how "wisely" he acted in a situation and solved a problem that he was facing. This will open the opportunity for you to give her a slice of your personal knowledge or wisdom to use later in similar situations. Also, you will be able to open a discussion with him, which is another healthy parenting tip.

Most of the parents do not let their kids do challenging tasks fearing their failure. This way of thinking may cripple them for life. Life is failure and success going side by side. And, a failure teaches a person more than success. However, parents often in the name of supporting their child make the mistake of helping them throughout a task and pulling them through it, fearing their failure. Parents want their child to succeed so that the child may be applauded.

Truly, parents love to praise their own kids, even to hear their kids being praised — call it a hangover from the self-esteem movement of the 1970s. But, praising kids for being smart rather than working hard pushes them into what Stanford researcher Carol Dweck calls a fixed mindset, one in which kids shy away from challenges.

INTERPRETATION SKILLS

According to Insight Assessment (IA), an organization based in San Jose, USA, that provides world leading assessments on reasoning skills and thinking mindset, "interpretation is the process of discovering, determining, or assigning meaning, and interpretation skills can be applied to anything, e.g. written messages, charts, diagrams, maps, graphs, memes, and verbal and non-verbal exchanges. People apply their interpretive skills to behaviors, events, and social interactions when deciding what they think something means in a given context."

Therefore, if adolescents have interpretation skill, it would be very powerful in helping them develop critical thinking. Interpretation generally goes through the three phases:

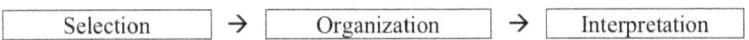

Selection → Organization → Interpretation

1. Selection

This is the first phase of the process through which we attend to some stimuli in our environment and not others. The world around us is filled with an infinite number of stimuli that we might attend, but our brains do not have the resources to pay attention to everything.

Therefore, the first step toward interpretation (usually unconscious, but sometimes intentional) is the decision of what to attend to. Depending on the environment, and depending on us as individuals, we might focus on a familiar stimulus or something new. When we attend to one specific thing in our environment — whether it is a smell, a feeling, a sound, or something else entirely — it becomes the attended stimulus.

2. Organization

Once we have chosen to attend to a stimulus in the environment (consciously or unconsciously, though usually the latter), the choice sets off a series of reactions in our brain. This neural process starts with the activation of our sensory receptors (touch, taste, smell, sight, and hearing).

The receptors transduce the input energy into neural activity, which is transmitted to our brains, where we construct a mental representation of the stimulus (or, in most cases, the multiple related stimuli) called a percept. An ambiguous stimulus may be translated into multiple percepts, experienced randomly, one at a time, in what is called "multistable perception."

3. Interpretation

After we have attended to a stimulus, and our brains have received and organized the information, we interpret it in a way that makes sense using our existing information about the world. Interpretation simply means that we take the information that we have sensed and organized and turn it into something that we can categorize. This category of organized information is our perception.

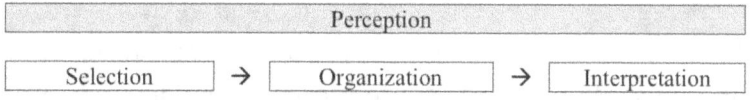

Parents need to understand and appreciate the fact that, by the time teenagers have interpreted, say, your refusal to let them continue their online game-playing activity with their friends and arrived at a perception that you are being "unfair," they have nothing personal against you.

Typically, they are in a "limbic state" also known as "emotional state," and parents often misinterpret or misunderstand them, because they are interpreting the situation mostly from their prefrontal cortex, as opposed to where the teens are interpreting the situation — mostly from the limbic system.

If parents would like to know why the child feels that you are being "unfair," the most natural thing you want to do is to question the youth about their "selection" and "organization" process. In so doing, parents can start to understand why and how the child reaches that inaccurate perception. This opens the door to their world, and parents can similarly choose to adjust their perception with the new information provided by the child. When parents persist with asking the questions first and try to question their child's "selection" and "organization," over a period of time, the teen gradually learns from and even emulates his parents, how they select and organize information to interpret, before making more responsible decisions or taking the more responsible actions.

EVALUATING INFORMATION

Evaluation of information is an important part of critical thinking. It develops during the academic life of adolescents. They learn how to evaluate information and with practice learn to perfectly use it in their daily lives.

According to a team of researchers at IDEA, a non-profit born out of Kansas State University, dedicated to improving student learning in higher education, "teaching teens 'how to think' may begin by alerting them to the kinds of questions and problems that interest them in their area of interest. So teachers and parents alike, may consider organizing their teaching when the opportunity arises, around such questions and problems to stimulate your child's intellectual interest. Rather than simply presenting information, be explicit with your child about how you would approach such questions, defining critical thinking in your own way and model disciplinary ways of thought. Engage your child in activities that require sophisticated thinking and design assessments that call on your child to demonstrate thinking skills."

How does the process of evaluating information actually take place? In fact, it is mostly about analyzing information from a critical perspective. An article found in Asbury University Kinlaw Library on critical evaluation of sources states that "to evaluate information is to analyze information from a critical perspective. The process requires us to step back and carefully consider the sources we use and how we use them, to not rush to judgment but to think through the content. We also need to consider the relationships among different sources and how they work together to form "conversations" around certain topics or issues. A "conversation" in this sense refers to the diverse perspectives and arguments surrounding a particular research question (or set of questions)."

The preceding information was presented in the context of evaluating content found online, addressing the same question about how we know what information to focus on, especially when there is plenty of false and inaccurate information. Similarly, during adolescence, our teens are bombarded with so much information from everywhere — social media, online videos, books, friends, even parents and teachers. How do we want them to evaluate all the information received and reach the point of using that information meaningfully and responsibly?

Evaluating information is a long process which takes the youth to a higher level of critical thinking. This process starts with all the questions starting with "W":

- Who did it?
- Why did it happen?
- When did it happen?
- Where did it take place?
- Which one is verified?
- What are the most important points?

These simple questions break the information into several bits and each answer helps dig out important information of an incident, issue, topic, etc., which leads to valuable findings.

Often, a little incident is easily ignored by the people, but if we follow it with all the "W" questions in your mind, we will find that this small incident actually was just the tip of an iceberg.

Teens who are in the process of learning can incorporate information evaluation in their thinking style and reap its benefits in their daily life and even later in their career. Of course, this enables them to think more like mature people and find out several facts about things which can help them succeed.

For example, if you find a freshly burned half cigarette on your driveway or corridor outside your apartment, and you never smoke, you might want to evaluate this little incident.

Find out the following with the help of your teenage kid:

- Who smoked here last night?
- Why is this cigarette here?
- When was it thrown there?
- Where did it come from?
- Which neighbors or visiting friends might have littered?
- What is the issue or problem with it?

After you have analyzed the available information in your mind, you will see that you most probably know who smoked and how the cigarette came onto your driveway or corridor. This may give you more information about say the behavior of your neighbors or any suspicious movement around your home.

Teens take interest in things that provoke their thinking. This style of simple start-up would definitely attract them to evaluate several pieces of information they find around them.

FORESIGHT

What is foresight? It is a wise view of the future and often entails understating what is going to happen. It does not actually mean when someone will get rich or buy a home, for example. But, it means having a probable idea of what will be the future of his or her academic pursuits, professional endeavors, career progression, family life, even the organization, ideology, technical development, an invention, etc.

As happened with Alan, how can Alan and anyone other than Alan gain foresight? Critical thinking skills are strongly interrelated and you can see that observation, interpretation, evaluation, and many other thinking skills work together to help someone achieve the ability of foresight.

> "Alan Hald, a young Arizona banker with a strong interest in the future, attended a World Future Society Conference in the 1970s. There he met the editor of a new magazine for computer hobbyists. At the time, nobody but governments and big businesses could afford to build a computer, but Hald had the foresight to see that the future of computers would be very different from the past, and many new business opportunities would open up. Hald went home in great excitement to talk to his partner about starting a business in computers. In the following years, Hald's business (MicroAge) grew into America's largest microcomputer distributor, serving dealers around the world."

According to the World Future Society, foresight is critical to success in all areas of our lives, including major life decisions. In contrast to Hald's success, people who lack foresight are only too likely to find themselves unemployed when jobs are unexpectedly lost to new technologies, competition from overseas, or shifts in consumer tastes. Without foresight, we often have little idea of what to do next, so developing our foresight may be the best way to safeguard our current jobs and future employability.

The World Future Society further asserts that foresight may also save our lives. They argue that as scientists are identifying more and more ways for us to live longer, healthier, and happier lives, we have to decide to follow their advice. People lacking foresight are only too likely to disregard the practices that would safeguard their future health and well-being. Millions of people are alive today because they paid attention when scientists confirmed the enormous damage that smoking cigarettes does to the human body. Meanwhile, their neighbors and friends who continued to smoke have succumbed to lung cancer, heart disease, and stroke.

Education is another area where foresight is important. The World Future Society found that students lacking foresight are more likely to neglect their studies because they see no connection between education and a successful future. But, students with good foresight skills can recognize the importance of studying and can also select the courses most likely to help them meet their goals. Young people who do not learn to think ahead may find it difficult to plan for a successful marriage and family life. People whose foresight is weak are likely to have difficulty saving money for emergencies, down payments on homes, and retirement.

The Systems Thinker, a resource website that archives published materials that can help expand the use of systems approach, managed to capture the "how-tos" when it comes to developing foresight, proposed by the World Future Society. The following are eight common techniques (for more detailed discussions about these techniques, one can read *Futuring: The Exploration of the Future*, by Edward Cornish, World Future Society (2005)):

1. **Scanning:** A systematic survey of current newspapers, magazines, websites, and other media for indications of changes likely to have future importance. This focuses mainly on trends — changes that occur through time rather than events. Changes that occur very quickly and generally are much less significant in understanding the future. Scanning is an ongoing effort to identify significant changes in the world.

2. **Trend Analysis:** This is a careful examination of a trend to identify its nature, causes, speed of development, and potential impacts. A trend can have many different impacts on different aspects of human life, and many of these impacts may not be apparent at first, like longer life spans. This means more resources must be provided, but it also means more people who can contribute to the economy and society through paid and unpaid labor.

3. **Scenario Development and Analysis:** Scenarios are ways to imagine future possibilities on the basis of what we know (or think we know). Scenarios are useful in helping us understand what might happen as a result of a decision we may make. For instance, parents may invite their teenager to imagine what would happen if he or she accepted a university's offer: What good and bad things might happen as a result of taking up that study course?

4. **Consulting Others (Polling):** This is about asking people with the subject matter expertise to advice or comment. Information or data may be collected through face-to-face conversations, telephone interviews, and questionnaires sent by electronic or ordinary mail. Delphi polling, popular among futurists, uses a carefully structured procedure to generate more accurate forecasts.

5. **Simulations or Gaming:** This helps to learn, anticipate, and prepare for situations in a safe, realistic, and meaningful way. In war games, real soldiers may become actors in a mock battle, which helps them understand what actual combat is like and helps generals test out alternative strategies and tactics that they may later use. These are extremely useful for limbic responders like our teenagers. It increases learner engagement, it makes learning fun and interactive, it improves knowledge absorption and retention, it gives learners the opportunity to see real-world applications, and it enhances the overall learning experience for all age groups.

6. **Historical Analysis:** History can always teach us something about our future, or what our future can be. Studying historical events enables us to anticipate the outcome of current developments. Even for teens, it would be useful to look at and compare the successes and failures of their favorite celebrity, an inspirational adult, even of parents themselves. If they are interested, they can analyze world events, like wars or climate change, and look into what can be learned from history to guide them in making decisions for themselves.

7. **Brainstorming:** The generation of new ideas by means of the family coming together to think creatively about a topic, such as a problem to be solved, an opportunity to capture, or

a direction to take in life. Family members or even friends coming together are encouraged to build on each other's ideas and withhold criticism. Brainstorming is useful in identifying possibilities, opportunities, and risks. Other idea-generating or problem-solving methods are also common, such as idea mapping, impact analysis, and the systematic identification of all possible variables. This is helpful to stretch the teens' minds beyond the present and to promote continuous innovation and long-term strategizing.

8. **Visioning:** Creating a vision or a visual of a desirable future for the teenager. This usually starts with a view of past events and the current situation, moving into the desirable vision, and then identifying specific ways to move toward the desired future. A visioning procedure often prepares the way for more formal goal setting and planning.

DIVERSITY

Finally, diversity in thinking boosts critical higher-level thinking for the youth. Though diversity is not important in thinking only, it has a great role in critical thinking. Experts insist on having diverse colors in life and thoughts both. After the introduction of the Internet and cultures coming into closer contact, diversity has become a stronger part of our lives and thoughts.

To think diversely needs the teens to get involved in diverse tasks, get to know things that are controversial, and know the diverse opinions of different people based on gender, religion, culture, and career; diversity in choices, decisions, perceptions, and everything is how this universe was created. Hence, the teens start thinking with a very broad mind that houses the diverse sides of several things. The need for diverse thinking for teens has emerged only recently.

From a study in the *Journal of College Student Development,* on the "Effects of Diversity Experiences on Critical Thinking Skills Over 4 Years of College," the researchers highlighted that the potential influence of involvement in diversity experiences during college on the cognitive and intellectual outcomes of post-secondary education is only beginning to be understood. However, there is a convincing argument for why exposure to diversity experiences might foster the development of more complex forms of thought, including the ability to think critically. Drawing on research that spoke to the social aspects of cognitive development, they pointed out that students will be more likely to engage in effortful and complex modes of thought when they encounter new or novel situations that challenge current and comfortable modes of thinking. This often can happen in classroom settings, but it can also occur in other contexts such as when students encounter others who are unfamiliar to them; when these encounters challenge students to think or act in new ways when people and relationships change and produce unpredictability; and when students encounter others who hold different expectations for them.

It was also highlighted that there were many other studies suggesting that exposure to racial and cultural diversity during college is significantly linked to such outcomes as student self-reported gains in "problem-solving," "critical thinking," "cognitive development," and "complexity of thinking." This is important initial work alerting scholars to the possibility that a considerable range of cognitive/intellectual growth during college might be fostered by a student's exposure to diverse experiences.

So, the circumstances are always in favor of students thinking diversely because diversity is available around them in their school, college, and even their family circle.

What is the role of teachers, parents, and counselors? First of all, they try to guide students on how to accept diversity in the first place. Second, they understand why things are diverse, what types of differences are there, etc. Third, they think and make decisions while fully acknowledging and accepting diversity.

Since the importance of training students on diversity has become popular recently, a question is mostly raised about how we can foster diversity in the thinking of students.

The Learning Scientists is a non-profit organization with cognitive psychological scientists interested in research on education. Their main research focus is on the science of learning. Cindy Nebel from the organization highlighted some of the strategies that promote diverse thinking and provide necessary tools to promote inclusivity:

- **Elaboration:** When we are talking about studying using elaboration, it involves explaining and describing ideas with many details. Elaboration involves making connections among ideas we are trying to learn and connecting the material to our own experiences, memories, and day-to-day life.

- **Retrieval practice:** This involves recreating something we learned in the past from our memory, and thinking about it right now. In other words, a while after we have learned something by reading it in a book or hearing it in a class or from a teacher, we need to bring it to mind (or "retrieve" it). This process of retrieving makes the information more retrievable later; compared to simply studying by looking over our notes, if we practice retrieval, we are more likely to remember the information later, and also more likely to be able to use and apply the information in new situations.

- **Dual Coding:** Students are encouraged to create both visual and verbal representations of the material they are learning. The key to this strategy is to develop multiple ways of thinking about the same material or issue. This type of thinking is again necessary for understanding and appreciating other viewpoints or cultures.

  Dual coding is the process of combining verbal materials with visual materials. There are many ways to visually represent material, such as with infographics, time lines, cartoon strips, diagrams, and graphic organizers.

  When we have the same information in two formats — words and visuals — it gives us two ways of remembering the information later on.

- **Concrete Examples:** Abstract ideas can be vague and hard to grasp. Moreover, human memory is designed to remember concrete information better than abstract information. To really nail down an abstract idea, we need to solidify it in our mind. We can do this by being specific and concrete.

SUMMARY

1. Critical thinking is a form of high-level thinking that is critical to helping youth make meaningful and responsible decisions. It is easier to train the youth in critical thinking early, when the brain has not reached the final stages of development.
2. Parents can facilitate critical thinking in youth using five strategies:
    i. Assigning tasks with varying challenges, such as imposing time and money constraints:
        a. Parents should help the youth understand their thought processes and decision-making, offering their own personal choices only when necessary.
        b. Refrain from overprotecting the youth from difficult challenges, or overpraising them.
    ii. Refining their interpretation skills by constantly challenging their *selection* and *organization* process.
    iii. Helping them analyze information more critically through probing questions in their areas of interest. Probe their thought processes using the "W" questions:
        1. Who did it?
        2. Why did it happen?
        3. When did it happen?
        4. Where did it take place?
        5. Which one is verified?
        6. What are the most important points?
    iv. Developing foresight using the eight intentional strategies:
        a. Trend analysis,
        b. Scenario development and analysis,
        c. Consulting others,
        d. Simulations or gaming,
        e. Historical analysis,

    f. Brainstorming,
    g. Visioning.
v. Increase exposure toward diverse thinking and perspectives:
    a. Parents, teachers, and counselors should help the youth accept and understand diversity and make responsible decisions.
    b. Four strategies toward increasing diverse thinking:
       1. Elaboration,
       2. Retrieval practice,
       3. Dual coding,
       4. Concrete examples.

Chapter 10

The Power of Presence

In this chapter, we will discuss where the true power lies. The power I am referring about is the ability to help our youth succeed, yet not stifle or shortchange them, enabling them to be the best version of themselves. If youth are able to achieve their fullest potential and impact the world around them positively, parents should be really proud of them regardless of whether they contributed to it or not. By now, we should be well informed that it takes a village to raise a child! While it is extremely important that parents play a key role, when youth succeed, it is also who they hang out with, where they spent most of their time, what they have been doing, and how they have been working toward their personal success.

Youth Engagement Matrix

Youth Emotional Dispositions	Limbic Strategies	Prefrontal Strategies
Positive Emotions	✓ Engage	✓ Engage
Negative Emotions	✓ Engage (Positively)	✗ Do not engage

During the course of my work, I have seen so many parents "sub-contracting" their roles to others, like grandparents, teachers, domestic helpers, neighbors, and childcare. What do I mean? Parenting is about teaching, nurturing, disciplining, supporting, and comforting our own children, biological or adopted. Some parents expect grandparents and even teachers to discipline their children in school. Parents may have several commitments at work or may be preoccupied with matters for the family. Consciously or unconsciously, their influence over the children may diminish and somebody else has a greater influence over the child. We always hope that the influence is a positive one.

DRE

Targeting Checklist

Developmental Relationship Elements	Check
V VOICE	✓
O SHOW	✓
I INSPIRE	✓
C CHALLENGE	✓
E ENCOURAGE	✓

The crunch comes when the influence is a negative one, and parents start to assert control. The influence may come from both peers of the teen and adults that the youth may know. This may manifest itself through negative behaviors like truancy, smoking, and fights.

The question is if parents really need to control their adolescents. Does control even stop our teens from playing truant, or stop smoking, or not getting into fights?

Parents need not think of "controlling" their teens. There are really other things which are more important than just controlling them like understanding, supporting, and developing bonds and family love, which bring better results. Those parents who think that they are responsible for controlling their kids actually make a mistake. They take a wrong track toward their adolescents' hearts and eventually lose not win.

Naturally, I hope parents can appreciate this reality that we cannot control our adolescents and what they are going to become as adults.

In fact, the adolescent period is a time of intense changes and the teens face immense challenges during this time. So, thinking of controlling them is a mistake and unrealistic. What parents and teachers can do during this period of life is to be open to talks and discussions, and be welcoming of the changes; to be present and accepting of what the adolescents are going through is a better way to handle them. This is good for both parents and teens.

You cannot control things. So, be present with your adolescents so that you can support them in the upcoming developmental changes.

I have been and will continue to discuss various ways to remain supportive and open with the adolescents throughout the changes and challenges they go through. In this period of life, the adolescents begin to experience the world very differently, like interacting with other adolescents, having immense physical changes, feeling strong when they start making decisions, and taking responsibilities.

Facing these changes and challenges is a difficult phase for the youth as they have to learn to maintain inner balance. They need the support of adults, not their controlling attitude. We, as adults, prefer our support in the form of being open about the changes and challenges happening, being responsive, and staying connected with the adolescents rather than correcting, commenting, criticizing, or controlling.

Dan Seigel in his book *Brainstorm* said, "if I had to summarize in one word all of the research on what kind of parenting helps create the best conditions for a child's and adolescent's growth and development, it would be the term 'presence.'"

Presence of parents, teachers, and other adults in the life of adolescents means being open to whatever they are going through and adjusting to it while keeping in touch with their mental depth. Hence, the importance at this time is to maintain an essential method to connect with their emotions and feelings. Eventually, we can see and feel them and make them feel safe, secure, and soothed. The essence of a healthy attachment and relationship is feeling for others. Eventually, when the connection is deep, we are able to assist them to feel safe, secure, and soothed.

THE EFFECTS OF BEING PRESENT AND CLOSE TO ADOLESCENTS

The Population Dynamics Research Center's website, maintained by the Population Reference Bureau's (PRB) Center for Public Information on Population Research (CPIPR), reported that when mothers spent more time engaged in different activities with their adolescent children (ages 12–18), the teens get less involved in criminal behavior, for example, skipping school, staying out at night without permission, shoplifting, and creating trouble at school or with the neighbors. The researchers found the following:

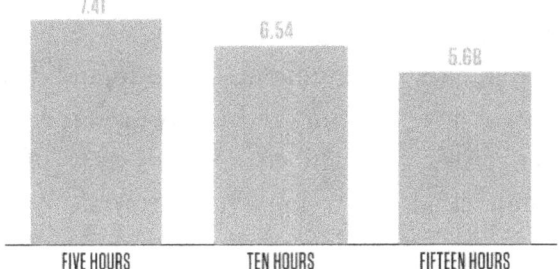

- On average, there were 7.41 delinquent behaviors within an average of 5 hours of engaged time with mother;
- One average, there were 5.68 delinquent behaviors within an average of 15 hours of engaged time with mother.

The findings also reveal the fact that when both parents spend more time with the adolescents in healthy activities, there were fewer behavioral problems, less substance abuse, higher math scores, and less criminal behavior among adolescents. In contrast, the research team found no strong relationship between the amount of time mothers spent with younger children (ages 3–11) and children's behavioral or emotional problems.

AVERAGE MAGNITUDE OF BEHAVIORAL PROBLEMS BY AVERAGE HOURS OF ENGAGED TIME WITH BOTH PARENTS FOR ADOLESCENTS AGES 12-18*

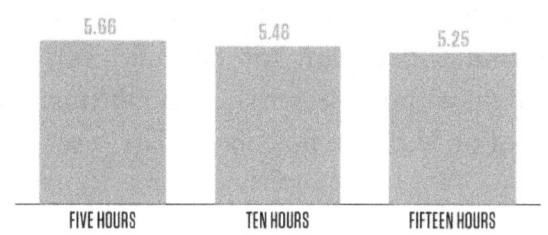

According to Science Daily, Irit Yanir from the University of Haifa, in the article "Close Families Raise More Independent Adults," reported that an "independent young adult is one who exhibits independence not only in his day-to-day life but also in the emotional sphere, and who makes his way in life with emotional and intellectual autonomy." The research found that following adolescence, the familial connection is an important factor in forming one's identity and living an independent life. It seems that not only can independence and closeness exist together but they actually flourish together.

A sense of parental presence is vital in all stages of adolescence. Parents should not think that their child is older and now he does not need them as much as he did when he was a child. This is not correct because the child may not need the parents for his physical needs after growing older and entering his late teens, but he needs them for his emotional needs, for his personality build-up, and his success in the future.

Things may not seem easy to parents when the kids enter the stage of later teen years, but that does not mean that parents leave the teens alone most of the times, feeling that they need space and time of their own. In fact, the adolescents appreciate parental time when their relationship is good and healthy with the parents, though they never ask for it.

So, staying present in the life of adolescents builds stronger adults who are good citizens and successful family members. The startling truth is that when parents develop a healthy and strong connection with their teens, they ensure that their kids will journey through their adolescence safely. There will be no violence with peers and no bitter experience of teen pregnancy. Eventually, the bigger fears like dropping out of school are also eliminated.

The tools that are mentioned in the previous chapter help the parents pave the way to a strong and almost spotless presence and support for their teens.

HOW TO KEEP PRESENT IN THE LIFE OF ADOLESCENTS

As mentioned above, the parents need to stay supportive and present in the life of adolescents to create

"the best conditions for a child's and adolescent's growth and development."

Often, parents misunderstand the idea of staying present in the life of adolescents. When their children get older, they start focusing on things that need to be changed in the eyes of parents.

They like to comment on behaviors that they think are not suitable and criticize the choice of teens, thinking that they are choosing something which is not good for their life as they have no experience. Slowly and gradually, they only address their adolescents with guiding tips and correcting comments and phrases. All these tactics have no encouraging, positive outcome and are not counted as being "present" in the life of teens.

Things the adolescents cannot complete or cannot improve are left with time to improve as the behavior of the teen gets more mature and more rational. When they find their parents more critical, they feel discouraged and would like to stay aloof from them. Here, the spirit of healthy adolescent growth and development dies. Parents are not required to focus on wrongdoings and unimproved behavior patterns.

No doubt, parents find difficulties in their relationship with their teens. Sometimes, they develop fears that things are not going right. There are signs that make them fear the failure of their kids or that the kids are not going toward success. Sometimes, they are worried that they are unable to be fully and in the right way present in the life of their adolescents.

These fears and worries are a natural process of healthy thinking, but they should not overpower you or cripple you from staying innovative. You need to keep going alongside your teen in his feelings and problems and support him in facing the changes and challenges of life in the best way possible.

Whenever you find yourself worried or paranoid, put more effort in your positive behavior, increase the quality of time you spend with your teens, improve your support, and bring about other good changes according to your lifestyle in your family time together. As the experts say, when you want to make a good cup of coffee, put more coffee in it. That is the simplest rule of making your presence stronger and of better quality. Your adolescents feel your positive input instinctively and feel comfortable and good with your efforts.

Here are the top five ways we recommend to keep present in the life of your teens.

1. Appreciate and *like what your teens love*
The adolescents love several things that you can also love and appreciate practically. The closest example is their friends. Do not show your resentment toward the social circle of your teens for simple differences that do not meet your criteria. Appreciate them for having friends and let them invite their friends at home while you are at home. This is a sign of how much you appreciate your kids' social circle.

You are not required to interact with their friends or entertain them; you just need to give permission open-heartedly to your kids to enjoy the company of their friends at home. This is highly protective and safe for them.

While they are enjoying a happy time together, they will not think of doing "dangerous" things for the simple fact that they are in your home. So, the fear of smoking pot or weed is completely out of question.

2. Fill in the Blank
You need to understand when your teens feel empty and needs company and lots of talking. This feeling of emptiness or

blankness as you can call it can make them feel sad or neglected or they can start thinking of drugs, alcohol, smoking, sex, etc. Do not leave them to their own devices to fill the emptiness inside them. Find time to talk about anything that interests them. There are several topics that teens love like parties, going out, playing pranks, new styles, fashion trends, little part-time jobs, funky apparel, etc.

Most of the time, it is late at night when the time is very suitable for you to fill in the blank. While searching for a midnight snack, you can meet your teen in the kitchen, grab the moment, and trigger a talk. You will be surprised by how much you can hear from her in the wee hours of the night.

But, this is not the only time to fill her heart with your talk. There are several other moments during the day when you can find a few minutes or even an hour to talk. This goes pretty well during the weekend.

Teens love to talk, to express what is in their minds, to suggest, to discuss, to tell stories, etc. Talking gives them immense pleasure and fills their hearts with a feeling of satisfaction.

What you need to do is to suggest interesting topics and listen more than you speak. Throughout the talk, keep adding fuel to the fire; add comments, show interest, smile, say words like the following:

"Really?"; "I am surprised!"; "Oh my God, that sounds so interesting!".

Always be interested during the talk sessions. If you frown over some specific things like what his friend did at a party or how they pranked the neighbors, most probably your teen will become cautious not to be honest about all the details. This can even avert him from talking.

From *Psychology Today*, Carl Pickhardt, a psychologist in private counseling and public lecturing practice in Austin, Texas, and author of *Who Stole My Child? Parenting Through Four Stages of Adolescence*, offers an easy formula for staying present with your teens:

"Talking + Listening = Connecting"

When you come to fill in the blank of the emptiness of your teen, do not push her to talk. This will make her resist because teens love their independence. And, one of their most favorite things to do is keep secrets. They do not like to tell their secrets to anyone, especially to older people like parents and teachers.

Teachers at schools can find time to talk easily as the adolescents are already available in the school and there are classes when talking is more important than just covering the syllabus. Teachers can open several topics and trigger important talks with teens. There is ample opportunity for an open discussion, expressing views and opinions. Kids at school give significant importance to their teachers. Hence, triggering talks or holding discussions greatly helps make the kids feel better and stay away from the emptiness that often irritates them.

3. Be *present body and soul*
Although the teens do not have a fully developed brain, their feelings are awake. They can sense if you are present with them body and soul or not. If your mind is away and you start a discussion, you will show signs of mental absence. The talking teen will sense

a sort of disinterest or think that you are ignoring her and at this point, she will decide to cease the talk. Always remember that teens are very sensitive and may be more sensitive than adults.

This is not true about talking only. This is true in every situation. Do not do for your teens anything unless you are fully in. Whether it is a trip to the supermarket or you are going for an autumn evening stroll, be with your teens with all the warmth and attention you have.

A few fully dedicated hours or activities with your teens will be highly influential in your parent–kid relationship. You can gain the trust of your kids and give them your quality time to stay connected.

4. Show *your appreciation*

Every adult can maintain strong connections with teens by appreciating their positive input in things. There are many times when teens put considerable effort into staying positive toward their responsibilities and the things we expect from them.

Whether you are a teacher, a mentor, a parent, or anyone who is in direct contact with adolescents, like a sports coach, a club head, or a trainer, you observe several times when teens show a positive attitude. Do not let such effort, though less, pass unnoticed. Mark it with your appreciation and let it be a powerful point to connect and stay present with the adolescents.

Use sentences such as the following:

> "We really appreciate you doing the homework that we specifically reminded you of!"

"I appreciate you making decisions, free of the influence of your friends."

"This is really wise of you to stay away from the trouble-making guys at school!"

These and many other moments in life really require you to show your appreciation of your teens.

You may have often heard the adolescents sorrowfully complain that their parents do not ever recognize what right actions they take in life. We never feel or try to feel how disappointing it is for the younger generation to show a positive attitude and go unnoticed.

Many times our ignorance toward our teens pushes them away from us. Our connections weaken and distance grows between us. Moreover, ignoring good effort does not give them a chance to grow and make bigger positive contributions toward their family and society.

Parents and teachers taking the route of advice, criticism, and pointing out mistakes make the adolescents believe they are nothing but a bundle of mistakes and misdeeds. Feeling inferior compared to the family members is a painful sense which we create in the hearts and minds of our teens by ignoring their positive contributions toward family and life. Continued negative notice eventually disconnects adolescents from family. Not valuing one's positive efforts is a clear message that he or she does not matter. So, express your happiness and appreciation for all the good deeds your adolescents do and all the bad that your adolescents avoid.

There is one thing of immense importance regarding appreciating adolescents. If you are their parent and do your part of appreciation often, it is well and good. The teens may still feel incomplete or feel as if they have not done very well in the society of others who do not appreciate them. Teachers, coaches, and other adults in the society with whom an adolescent comes into direct contact also matter.

Adolescents can frequently think that parents appreciate them because they are the parents. But, when appreciation comes from someone outside the family, it really feels good. It has a deeper impact on someone's mind and heart. Adolescents who receive appreciation from different adults grow into stronger, confident adults who strive for good and positivity.

When we come to talk about the challenges and changes that adolescents go through during their growing and developing stage, this is one of the challenges to do good and avoid wrong. We help them get through this challenge successfully when we appreciate them. We keep them feeling strong with our supportive words.

Another part of appreciation is to accept your child or your student as he is after growing out of his childhood and entering his teens.

"You used to be a better and more responsible kid when you were smaller!"

This sentence from a parent or teacher can be more destructive than constructive.

We understand that adolescence induces changes in the thoughts and feelings of teens. This eventually shows in behavior and not all changes are negative and need to be criticized.

You become used to the child that was with you and his innocent submissiveness. So, it is harder for you to accept and continue feeling affectionate as you always did toward your changed teen. It is more practical for you to object and correct. But, does it lead to a strong and healthy parent–child or teacher–student relationship?

Everyone can easily understand that it does not. But, still, we choose this behavior and continue lashing out at our teens with our objections. Silently, the distances grow, and instead of connecting, you disconnect with your adolescents.

Don't you often find parents complaining that their teenage kid no longer cares for what they say? And, that he is growing more and more arrogant and ignorant about what the family wants? Hearing this, we declare that the teens of today are the worst generation you have ever witnessed. Then, you start recalling your childhood and making exaggerated claims of how good you were with your parents and teachers. A sense of bitterness toward adolescents gets cemented in our minds; more distance comes into existence and parents feel sad about their kids.

Does this have any basis or any reason to happen?

Absolutely not! All the problems started from the point when you refused to accept the fact that your child is growing older and his mind is going through certain changes. Of course, it is natural that he does not behave like a submissive child anymore. He is growing older and he is responding toward life as a growing adolescent.

The moment adults give themselves pause to think and realize what is going on with their adolescents, how they are behaving as parents, and how they should behave like adults, they are able to tweak their behavior with their teens.

5. Understand *your teens' rejection*
How do you feel when you call your teen and invite him to go out and play tennis?

"I do not want to now. I don't feel like it."

Or, you call him for a talk while you are sitting comfortably in the lounge enjoying the peace of your home.

"I can't now. I am going out with a friend, he wants to buy a new skating kit."

You feel disappointed and think that your teen is rejecting your invitation while you as his father are doing your best to keep him active, involved, and present.

Your adolescent is just not in a position to comply with your words and to indulge in the activity you want now. This is nothing offensive and it should not be looked upon as being rude or inconsiderate.

Your open-hearted acceptance of his rejection has good effects on him. In fact, he feels great that you have understood him, especially if you did not lash out at him in anger.

The same is true when you talk about a certain thing and your adolescent refuses to understand you. He just does not accept your idea because there is something bothering him. Either he is worried about something or uncomfortable or dislikes something.

For example, you offer to go for a family picnic with the family of your brother. You feel that it will be a great idea to enjoy some larger family company and spend some time out. If your teen refuses to go with you, do not feel offended. Try to find out what is the real reason for his refusal.

He may be worried about doing something that would eventually make his uncle laugh at him or feel angry.

He may be uncomfortable accompanying you because he is avoiding your niece who is slightly older than your son and he does not want to be there when she is around.

He might dislike going to the place you have chosen to go and does not want to go there.

If you find out the reason, try to respect his choice, especially when it not offensive or rude. You may not be able to imagine the positive impact of your understanding instantly because you are angry with his rejection. But, take it easy, breathe deeply, and take your time to think it over and realize that there is nothing bad if you accept his reason.

Try to come up with another choice for a family picnic with a discussion with your kids and wife. Give them all a chance to suggest what they feel comfortable with. You can reach a unanimous decision after a short discussion.

SUMMARY

1. Parents have a natural tendency to assert control over their teens' lives based on prefrontal considerations, which is often

unrealistic of them and increases the teens' inclination to distance themselves from parents with their limbic considerations.
2. Youth undergo a difficult phase of challenges and changes, and require their parents to be supportive, accepting, and present in their lives to overcome the phase.
3. Youth with parents who are more present in their lives are often less involved in delinquent actions.
4. As youth grow older, they rely on their parents for more emotional needs as compared to physical needs.
5. There are five strategies to help parents remain present:
    i. Appreciate and like what your youth loves.
    ii. Fill the blanks for them.
    iii. Be present in body and soul.
    iv. Show your appreciation.
    v. Understand your teen's rejection.

Chapter 11
Learning What Does Not Work

As we know now, adolescents are blind to logic and consequences, especially when their emotions are engaged. This has implications. Adults sometimes need to remind the adolescents about their future and the consequences of misbehaving, for example, not studying hard. Adolescents often turn a deaf ear to their teachers' or parents' advice, and simply continue happily doing whatever it is that draws them into it limbically — gaming, parkour, being with friends, chatting, etc.

To come close to getting the adolescent to be willing to consider with you the consequence of, say, not studying hard, one may consider engaging with the adolescent in gaming first, before talking about anything else. Alternatively, engage with the adolescent in a common topic of interest. This would accelerate the rapport building and enter into a limbic engagement through which the consequences of not studying could be communicated and taught. This is called catching them at *their blindside*.

Doesn't this all show that teens are dramatic? Yes, to us they look like they are, but in fact, the reality says they are spontaneous! Neuroscience gives sufficient explanations.

In order to answer this question, we just need to remember the fact that teens' limbic system is more active than the prefrontal cortex which is home to logic. So, our best bet with adolescents is emotions and not logic.

Actually, we, the adults, make the mistake several times of using logic with teens. This is the point where we part ways with no possibility of mutual understanding.

SO, HOW SHOULD WE INTERACT WITH THE TEENS?

The experts have different opinions. Let us see what Carl Pickhardt, psychologist in private counseling and public lecturing practice in Austin, Texas, and author of 15 parenting books as well as books on illustrated psychology, young adult and children's fiction, has to say:

> "During this more intense period of growth, it is helpful for parents (through example and instruction) to help their adolescent learn to manage emotions in ways that work well and not badly for all concerned, always remembering that now is later.
>
> The adolescent is just an adult in training, and the tools for emotional management learned with parents will be carried forward into significant relationships later on. "I learned to shut up about my feelings living with my parents, and now in marriage, my wife complains I refuse to open up with her." It's easier to form habits than it is to break them.
>
> Parents need to model safely talking out hard feelings, not acting them out by exploding to let off steam, to get their way, or to counter the teenager exploding at them. Yelling to stop teenage yelling only encourages more yelling."

We can see that Pickhardt is offering some good suggestions on how to deal with adolescents while knowing that their responses are rather emotional and not logical. The important thing he said was that "it is helpful for parents (through example and instruction) to help their adolescent learn to manage emotions."

How parents can help?

Pickhardt gave some advice:

"Having good emotional access and the ability to talk about feelings is really important in adolescence when periods of emotional duress are just part of the normal teenage passage. Consider some common emotional hard times."

So, he wants parents to nurture the ability to talk about feelings. Previously, he said the following:

"Parents need to model safely talking out hard feelings.

This method is long-lasting as adolescents learn in an acceptable manner how to discuss their feelings and not suppress them. Suppressing feelings makes it more difficult for the teens to explain what they want and what they are going through. Subsequently, it is more difficult for them to listen to the parents and comply with their instructions while they cannot even express their feelings and share them.

One obvious benefit of "safely talking out hard feelings" is that it builds the sense of security and trust in the hearts of adolescents. Once they are encouraged to share their feelings, they feel the warmth and strength of their family relations. This is the point when parents can expect their teens to listen and comply in a better way than before.

MIRROR NEURONS AT WORK

Now, let us see what Sheryl Feinstein has to say. She is an Associate Professor at Augustana College in Sioux Falls, South Dakota, where she teaches in the Education Department. Feinstein consults at a correctional facility for adolescent boys and at a separate site for emotionally and behaviorally disturbed adolescents in Minnesota. She is also the author of a number of books, including *Secrets of the Teenage Brain* and *Inside the Teenage Brain*.

Here, we discuss Feinstein's theory about mirror neurons, which she mentioned as follows:

"One of the most exciting new discoveries in neuroscience is that of mirror neurons. The very nature of mirror neurons is found in their name: Neuroscientists discovered that a network of neurons fired when they vicariously experienced something; it was as though another person's action was reflected in a mirror. The same parts of the human brain were activated in the observer as the neurons in the person doing the activity."

She also added the following:

"Some of the most recent and far implicating neuron discoveries were made by Marco Iacoboni, a neurologist, neuroscientist, and professor of psychiatry and biobehavioral sciences at the David Geffen School of Medicine at UCLA. He conducted pioneering research on mirror neurons, aptly named due to their reference to people's ability to learn through observation. Mirror neurons are a subset of neurons in the brain that have the capability to fire when they observe someone else kicking a football, drinking a beer, or feeling sad. When Jack breaks up with Ella, mirror neurons allow you to feel her pain vicariously.

Mirror neurons are shedding light on how we learn to imitate behaviors, speech, and thought. They are also bringing understanding of how we make moral decisions and learn empathy. Interestingly, we do not consciously decide to activate mirror neurons; instead, we are often unaware and powerless as they automatically produce imitations."

Actually, this theory, if applied in dealing with adolescents, can help build better relationships with the teens. Also, they act better and most probably in a way that is presented to them because of mirror neuron theory.

Finally, Vilayanur Ramachandran, Neuroscientist, Professor and Director at the Center for Brain and Cognition, University of California, San Diego, and author of *The Tell-Tale Brain*, theorized that mirror neurons can help in spreading culture:

> "Mirror neurons might help explain a wide variety of human social abilities. For example, how biologically do people imitate the actions of others, an ability that in part enables the spread of culture? Mirror neurons translate an observed action into a series of commands for the muscles to execute. How do people understand the intentions behind another's actions? Mirror neurons may run a sort of virtual reality simulation of what it would be like for oneself to perform that action. Why are autistic individuals impaired when it comes to understanding the thoughts of others?

On the blog of The Graduate School of Arts and Science at Harvard University, an article highlighted Ramachandran's work and further mentioned the following:

"Giacomo Rizzolatti, the original discoverer of mirror neurons in macaques, now suggests that mirror neurons might only be required for understanding the actions of others from a first-person perspective. He explains that this internalization of behaviors we see might provide us a deeper level of understanding about another person's goals, but cedes that mirror neuron activity might only constitute one among several ways of comprehending others' behavior."

Additionally it states the following:

"Their activity may still play an important role in many behaviors. For instance, even Gregory Hickok, professor of cognitive science at University of California, Irvine, where he directs the Center for Language Science and the Auditory and Language Neuroscience Lab, perhaps the most prominent critic of the hype surrounding mirror neurons, accepts that they probably play a role in enabling imitation, given that there must be some mechanism in the brain that converts an observed action to a series of muscle commands."

When mirror neuron can help in spreading culture, they can definitely help in spreading certain social behaviors among a family. Therefore, in very simple words, we can say that when parents act calmly, with a lot of love and care defining their behavior, their teen kids will imitate them because of mirror neuron theory.

When the parents yell, express anger, doubt their kids, and show distrust, the kids will reflect the same.

At the beginning of this chapter, we discussed catching the teens at their blindside. This theory can work for short-term results, for example, at the start of the day, we have a good talk with our kids, involve with them in an activity they love to share with us, and show our strong bonds with them through sharing interests.

After a good deal of fun times and doing together anything that they love, we have them ready to listen to us about something we want from them. For example, we want them to help around the home over the weekend by cleaning their rooms, bathrooms, mowing the garden, getting some groceries from the market, etc. Usually, kids refuse to be involved in such boring things over the weekends. However, we want them to do so for a number of good reasons. So, the theory of catching the teens at their blindside works the best here.

As far as the theory of mirror neuron is concerned, we find it very helpful for long-term behavior correction.

We adults can spread calmness, love, care, and friendliness in the home environment with our behavior. By dealing with our kids in the same way we want them to deal with us, we can shape their social behavior.

PHILOSOPHICAL VS. NEUROLOGICAL APPROACH

Pickhardt offers a more philosophical approach and suggests sharing feelings. He emphasizes the concept of talking — not one side talking but shared discussions and opening up about what troubles us deep inside.

When our teens learn and are bold enough (because of our encouragement, of course) to express their feelings, more than half of the problems are solved. We can deal with them more easily and they also can find an easy solution to their troubles by sharing them and talking about them.

We can see that different situations and different teens need a variety of theories. Hence, we can incorporate positivity in our behavior through a number of different ways.

As parents or teachers, we mostly need to develop positive thoughts toward our teens. This is the first important thing before any other tactic.

A serious problem is that negativity with adolescents can go farther than just not studying or doing their homework. If the parents do not take quick notice of their troubled teens, the situation can become very drastic both for the teens and the parents. The importance of talk and discussing feelings cannot be understated to let the teens open up and express themselves rather than suppress their emotions.

Another implication relating to adolescents being blind to logic and consequences is that adolescents can become susceptible to negative influence when their emotional doors are open. A very good example is adolescents joining gangs. If they do not feel like they belong in school or if they were unsupervised after school because their teachers do not engage or understand them, and their parents are nonchalant or busy at work, they would easily join, say, a street gang if someone from the gang were to chance upon him after school, in a mall maybe, and invite him to join the gang. The chances of him joining the gang would be quite high, especially when the gang can provide him with what he is seeking.

The adolescent would feel a greater sense of belonging in the gang than in school and would feel more secure in the gang than at home. The gang members could offer companionship and great empathy for the adolescent. They could offer protection, money, and even other material resources if the adolescent needed it. All these could make the adolescent feel valued, cherished, accepted, even loved and cared for. Furthermore, they would feel unrestrained, and have lots of freedom to do whatever they want and like to do; it's exciting, fun, and thrilling, to say the least.

At the same time, if the adolescent was invited to conduct some activities on behalf of the gang, like collecting protection money, being the runner for one of the gang members who illegally lends money, or even picking up a fight with a rival gang, the chances of the adolescent obliging and accepting the invitation are quite high again, because of all the benefits the adolescent has already obtained from the gang. That sense of loyalty, gratefulness, and relation toward the gang and its members may be really strong.

Additionally, if the adolescent did a reasonably good job, like collecting a significant amount of protection money, pulling off a threat against the borrower for the illegal moneylender, and winning a street fight against a rival gang, the adolescent may be glorified and recognized for his efforts and achievements, and probably encouraged to do more and better.

The stage that adolescents are at is extremely productive, and the involvement of youth with gangs and in negative activities can have lifelong impacts on their minds and personality. In the book *Inside the Teenage Brain*, Feinstein wrote as follows:

"Neuroscientists have discovered there is an overproduction of dendrites and synaptic connections during adolescence. By the end of adolescence, the brain contains more than 100 billion neurons and another 1,000 billion support cells. The 100 billion neurons form more than 1,000 trillion connections with each other — more than all of the Internet connections in the world.

Academically, adolescence is a prime time to tap into a person's potential. Short-term memory increases by 30 percent during adolescence, which leads to increases in intelligence, reasoning, and problem-solving ability. Talented athletes and musicians also develop, strutting their stuff on the field or in the concert hall.

(The difference in ability between the ninth-grade band, where the trumpet section ends a piece one measure behind everyone else, and the senior band that evokes emotion and demonstrates the technique is palpable.)

Do these improvements mean that teens should spend all their time engaged in formal learning? Probably not. Still, at this critical time in development, the more time that is dedicated to reading, writing, math, music, and sports, the better the brain that is built."

We can encourage the adolescents to be involved in healthy activities so that they become familiar with positivity and their brains develop in a healthy and normal manner.

The experts have suggested some useful tips on how to deal with adolescents in order to help them grow into positive, healthy adults.

In fact, the brain is ready to learn because it is sensitive to anything that an adolescent experiences. Megan Herting, Behavioral Neuroscientist with expertise in neurodevelopment, Assistant Professor of Preventive Medicine with a joint appointment in Pediatrics at Children's Hospital Los Angeles, said the following:

> "Given the tremendous amount of remodeling that goes on during adolescence, the brain may be especially sensitive to experiences, both good and bad.
>
> The neuron mirrors are especially important during the youth age. Their life is focused on social activities. Hence, they are learning to develop a feeling and be sensitive, to care for things like sadness, pleasure, achievement, etc. and to feel compassionate towards several issues of life. These things will help them in the future to deal with social challenges successfully."

Experts have discovered through research and study that adolescents who are positively socially active (not involved with gangs) and have many friends have stronger mirror neurons that are highly active because of imitation. Their brains had the opportunity to keep busy in understanding others' thoughts, actions, emotions, etc. In this period, if the teens find an opportunity to be with a role model, they will follow his pursuit and imitate his actions without realizing it. This can be the easiest way to influence them positively and help them grow mentally healthy, stable, productive, and positive.

This time of their life is marked by easy learning. They learn fast and without any difficulty. The brain's ability to learn many things like a new language, a skill, a concept, or a method is unparalleled. That is why schools offer second languages to students.

If we see the child from the start of his life, we find that his brain development keeps going through several different stages from the start of his birth. Newborn babies need to bond with their parents strongly during the first two years of their life. Hence, they grow socially healthy and active.

Neglected or abused babies have attachment disorder problems. Most of them fail in school and are engaged in criminal activities. From birth, the brain is active in learning, but it enters an especially active stage with the start of the adolescent years.

THINGS WE CONSIDER OFFENSIVE

Looking at the adolescent within the capacity of their developing brain is often impossible for the adults. There are several things that are pretty normal at the hands of adolescents, but we never look at those things with an understanding eye. For example, it is common for teens to misunderstand and misinterpret.

Most of the serious issues arise between adults and adolescents when adults get offended by teenagers' misunderstanding. Hence, adults regard them as arrogant, misbehaved, rude, deviant, etc. Meanwhile, the matter only needs a cool temper and some more discussions and elaborations of the matters until an adolescent is able to figure out what the topic of concern is and how he should understand it.

You will be surprised to know that the experts suggest that it is okay to let your adolescents have the last word in an argument.

They need more love and attention from their parents rather than instructions and orders.

Parents who put up with the disagreeable behavior of adolescents are able to understand the energy in the teens and let them take part in the decision-making process, thereby enjoying a happier life together and fostering healthy kids.

Let us see what does not work with adolescents here, and what does work with adolescents in the following chapter.

THINGS THAT DO NOT WORK

There are certain techniques that every parent loves to use, but miserably fails to get the result he yearns for. Despite failing, adults do not change those techniques, but blame the adolescents that there is something wrong with them. Given below are such techniques:

Lecture

This is the favorite of parents. Lecturing perfectly fits in the category of techniques that never work. Parents find it tempting to deliver a long lecture and impart lots of information to the teenager. Eileen Kennedy-Moore, author and clinical psychologist, based in Princeton, New Jersey, has the following to offer:

> "The problem is that lectures don't work. Educational researchers have known for years that students learn better from active engagement with a topic than from lectures. Similarly, research on parenting shows that lecturing, nagging, scolding, and talking at children or teens do not inspire cooperation. It never

feels good to hear, especially at length, how displeased someone is with us and the many ways we fall short of expectations. When lectures are long and frequent, kids are likely to respond by feeling defensive or resentful, and they just stop listening."

Eileen Kennedy-Moore is the professor for an audio-video series from The Great Courses, called Raising Emotionally and Socially Healthy Kids. Her most recent book for children is *Growing Friendships: A Kids' Guide to Making and Keeping Friends*. She has also written or co-authored four other books for parents.

If lectures and knowledge could make their lives easier, the adolescents would not have to go through so much disappointment and trouble while growing up.

You can observe that while you deliver a lecture, you do not have the attention and interest of your audience. You may find your adolescents yawing or rolling their eyes like they cannot believe you. You try to drag their attention to your "valuable lecture" and ask them the following:

"Look at me when I am talking."

But, you know, it still doesn't work!

Pestering

Pestering is another failed technique that we frequently use. The surprising fact is that we believe that our kids would appreciate later that we persisted with them in doing or not doing something. But, the sad reality is different. The adolescents get aggravated from nagging and develop a kind of defense against nagging.

So, nagging and pestering even for the sake of the noblest deeds do not work. We just need to realize that it is useless!

Tim Lott, a parent and parenting columnist at *The Guardian*, candidly wrote the following:

> "We are drunk on the confessional culture, but this does not leave much room for protecting each other's space. And this is one of the key elements of teenhood: the appropriation of space — emotional, physical and intellectual — from the adult.
>
> We do not want to let go of our children. We can be as reliant on them as they are on us. To refuse to talk to us is to say, "You do not occupy the prime position you once did in my life."
>
> And that is painful. So we pester them to communicate, which just pushes them further into the realm of self-imposed isolation.
>
> Of course you should be there for your children — particularly if you are one of those relatively rare adults who has the ability to listen to what is being said (and not said) with sensitivity and understanding and, furthermore, respond in a manner that allows the teenager to take that advice on board without being humiliated.
>
> You only get so many chances — once you disappoint your children with your inability to "get" them, they will quite quickly give up on the whole process.
>
> We all want to be the wise parent dispensing the wisdom of ages to our grateful progeny.
>
> However, I suspect the best we can do is leave ourselves open. Not tug at their guts so that they will spill them, but simply let

them know you are a safe space in which they can find comfort if they so wish. And if your children do not so wish, then so be it. Get over it — it's more your problem than theirs."

Improper Timing

Every adult feels so important and dominant that he starts talking about something important at any time. Without thinking about what the teenager is busy with or what is most important for him at the moment, a grown-up talks and wants the utmost attention of the listener. The teen may be busy in planning a project, messaging his friends, or anything which is far more important to him than listening to anything else.

This is just the wrong way to communicate. Instead, you can fix a time with the agreement of your kid and then talk and discuss whatever subject you find important.

Otherwise, your conversation will have no meaning or importance for your teen. Rather, he will find it unpleasant because you are dragging him out of his interest zone and away from something he is very busy with.

This is quite obvious and we keep this in mind when we talk to the adults, too. We find a proper time to discuss subjects of importance.

Arguing

Do you know that arguing with teens is pointless? Scientifically, arguing and quarreling with teens does not bring about any good. Teens communicate from their part of the brain, which is about emotions, while you communicate from the logic section of your brain. The ultimate result is that you both never meet on a mutual point. Moreover, teens have lots of points in their favor and unending energy to argue for long.

So, you can see that two sides completely different in their approach and basis of thinking are arguing. Will they end up understanding each other?

Instead, be precise and say what you want to say in good words and leave it to the brain of the child to process your words. The background of your relationship and your overall behavior with him will play the most important role here in making him comprehend what you just said.

Attacking and Guilt-Trapping

Feinstein in her book *Inside the Teenage Brain* highlighted the following:

> "Ruling with guilt, withholding love, and making personal attacks is psychologically detrimental to the teen. Even if teenagers use these techniques on you all the time, you should not respond in kind.
>
> When adults resort to mean-spirited behavior, the ramifications for teens are serious. Their adolescents need for love and security are not met. Unkind words contribute to unhealthy development almost as much as does physical abuse.
>
> The father who calls his son a loser or his daughter a slut cuts deep. Depression and antisocial behavior are the remnants of such psychological abuse."

Finally, from an advocacy blog site More4Kids, the article "Understanding Guilt and its Effects on Children" aptly mentioned the following:

> "The real feeling of guilt means to be immobilized in the present over something that has already occurred. It is a negative and confidence-crushing feeling. Guilt is a tool used by adults to make other people feel bad. We tend to use it more on children because we think that it is a good way to control their behavior.
>
> I understand that your intention is merely to control your child and put a halt to whatever they are doing that is causing trouble, but using guilt can cause more internal and external social problems within your child for years to come."

SUMMARY

1. Catching youth at their *blindside* is often necessary before getting them to consider hard advice or logic. This limbic engagement can happen by engaging in an activity or conversation of their choice.
2. Parents need to cultivate the idea that talking about hard feelings can be done safely. This is done by encouraging the discussion of feelings, acknowledging them, and responding calmly.
3. The brain consists of mirror neurons which facilitate the imitation of observed behaviors. Youth learn positive behaviors when parents display such behaviors.
4. Positive engagement is necessary for the youth to open up. Communicating negatively with youth will only cause them to seek external sources for their emotional needs, which leaves them open to bad influences.

5. In trying to elicit more positive behaviors, parents commonly engage in techniques that can be counterproductive for the youth. The techniques to avoid are as follows:
   a. Lecturing,
   b. Pestering,
   c. Improper timing,
   d. Arguing,
   e. Attacking and guilt-tripping.

Chapter 12
Things That Work

So, nothing works with teens? Certainly, there are things that work perfectly fine with teens. When we talk about those things that work with them, the first thing we say is LOVE. Yes, they need unconditional, honest love from their parents. They need parents' support, care, presence, and they need to have a deep trust in their parents that at the time of difficulty, they will stand by them. So, you need to make it clear through your entire life and actions to them that yes, you will be there for your teens whenever they need you. Combine your tolerance, rules, good expectations, and love. Your teens will always be there to respond positively.

Youth Engagement Matrix

Youth Emotional Dispositions	Limbic Strategies	Prefrontal Strategies
Positive Emotions	✓ Engage	✓ Engage
Negative Emotions	✓ Engage (Positively)	✗ Do not engage

DRE
Targeting Checklist

Developmental Relationship Elements	Check
V VOICE	✓
O SHOW	✓
I INSPIRE	✓
C CHALLENGE	✓
E ENCOURAGE	✓

The methods of dealing with teens that work are as follows.

KEEP COMMUNICATION OPEN

Understanding, support, and love start with communicating with the teens and listening to them. The only way teens gain the trust of their parents is through communication which is all about discussing, talking, and conversing.

However, you are not very fortunate in this option. In fact, teens' skills of conversation and communication are not good at this stage of life. Moreover, they hide most of the things in their life and do not like to talk about them with any adult. They mostly display a colourful attitude that they create on their own.

Another thing that naturally hampers teens' ability to communicate is their underdeveloped prefrontal cortex. Their amygdala is in control and they misread the emotions on people's faces. It is mostly in the hands of the adults, especially the parents, to ease a situation and comfortably bring the teens into a habit of good communication despite the difficulties they face due to their own brain.

Here is a brief and simple explanation from Patty Wipfler, Founder, Program Director, and Trainer at Hand In Hand, a non-profit organization in Palo Alto, California, that aims to support parents with the insights, skills, and tools necessary to build the meaningful connections that parents and children need to thrive. Wipfler describes how you can practically enhance communication between you and your teens:

> "Young people are constantly sorting things through and can use our help if we make ourselves unobtrusively available to listen. This means "hanging around." It may mean watching TV with your son, bringing your magazine or the mending into his room and plopping down on his bed to quietly do your work while he does his homework. It may mean sitting in the bathroom with your daughter and watching her or helping her while she applies her makeup. It may mean showing an interest in her newest nail polish color and spending time listening to her favorite rock or rap group.
>
> Usually, the questions we ask our teenagers are questions that arise from our fears, suspicions, or curiosities. They can tell when we want to know something because we are upset or anxious. So listening to build trust does not involve directing the conversation in any way. It's often just being around, willing to listen if a young person wants to talk.

When your child begins to talk, stay interested and delighted in him. Most likely, the subject of the conversation would not be anything you consider important. Remember this: your child has chosen a subject he feels safe talking to you about.

In your mind, you will be waiting for a subject of importance to you to surface. You may want your son to talk about why he is getting a D in geometry, or your daughter to talk about how badly she felt that she wasn't chosen to be a cheerleader. However, what your child can safely talk about is which CD he wants to buy next, or whether or not she should streak her hair. Hang in there!

If you listen well to your child, he will move to topics that are harder to approach. The longer you listen with interest and quiet approval, the safer it will get. A conversation about rap artists can turn into a talk about cliques at school, and how they have hurt your son. A long talk in the bathroom while trying to make a new hairdo can become a good cry about how unacceptable your daughter feels. You would not know where the conversation that seems so petty to you will lead. Trust that your child is gathering safety as you listen. Over days and weeks, safety will build if you continue to be pleased, interested, and quiet about your reactions."

In her book *Inside The Teenage Brain*, Feinstein addresses the issue about why teens misinterpret so many things and why there are numerous misunderstandings with them. We can appreciate better now that teens rely heavily on the emotional part of their brain, and this applies to even interpreting body language. Researchers surmise that interpreting body language is a learned skill; it is not something we inherit. Teens are in the process of learning what the smirk, the shrug, and the stare mean.

Therefore, how does this play out in real life? When a parent stares at a teen while waiting for an answer, the teen interprets it as though the parent is furious. In the school lunchroom, a girl across the room turns her head in the other direction and another teen interprets it as a signal that no one else is welcome at the table. Feinstein explained with the following:

> "In the teen, the amygdala, not the frontal lobes, is in charge, which makes conversations potentially volatile. A calm comment is met with a storm of verbal abuse. An innocent question by the parent, such as "Are you wearing that shirt?" sets off a stream of tears and foot stomping, as a teenager bawls in response, "You think I'm fat. I hate you!" Because adolescents are such emotional communicators, it is easy to make light of their problems."

The following are communication tips for conversing with teens:

- Listen to him or her more than you talk.
- Begin statements with "I" instead of "you" to diminish defensiveness.
- Be open to learning from your teenager and let him or her instruct you sometimes (computers are a wonderful conduit for this).
- Stay focused on his or her conversation and resist the temptation to interrupt with your own stories.
- Accept his or her opinions and ideas even when they differ radically from yours.
- Be an active listener and periodically ask questions to show interest.
- Match your emotional state to his or her emotional state (unless it is hostile). If he or she is down, do not try to perk him or her up with bubbly optimism.

- Show empathy and identify with his or her point of view.
- Withhold advice unless he or she asks you for it (the less you offer, the more he or she will ask).
- Allow him or her to discuss whatever topic he or she wants.
- Think before you speak, especially if you are discussing a sensitive issue.
- Be pleasant and stay positive or else walk away.
- Avoid generalizations.
- Ask questions that require more than a one-word response.

Last, but not least, find a good place to talk. A conversational setting can make a difference. Going out for ice cream or to dinner sets the stage for a pleasant talk. Going for a drive in the car — a popular activity for adolescents — can set a tone of conciliatory fun. Besides being neutral territory, you have a captive audience and nobody has to face the other, which may lend a level of comfort to the conversation. (But remember, neither you nor your child can walk out on this conversation, so choose your words wisely!)

BE SUPPORTIVE

Teens always want to be sure that they can find support from their parents when a tough situation comes their way. Of course, they are poor in making good decisions because of their underdeveloped prefrontal cortex. Hence, they can easily be drawn to risky behavior. So, they definitely need a safety net at such points in their life. Wipfler suggested the following:

> "In order to build new bridges between our children and ourselves, we have to learn to stay thoughtful and supportive through the worst of their feelings about us.

We have to keep letting them know that, no matter how they feel about us, we love them and want their lives to be good. We will stand by them, no matter what.

Your child needs to cry and rage his tension away. And if you stay, without reproach, you will be right there when he begins to recover his perspective. You will have passed the test, you cared about him when it was very tough to care when he was telling you to get lost."

The example of Matt and Bill would explain this point here. These two teens were friends and were caught for smoking pot. The boys were taken to the court and their families were extremely upset. When the boys exited the courtroom, Matt's father leaned over and said two things to Matt:

"You are a good kid and I will help you come out of this."
"You have to listen to me."

The other teen Bill was an orphan and his mother was not educated enough to support him or guide him. He got the punishment and kept defending himself alone.

Matt got full support from his father and had an entirely different life than Bill. He grew up to be successful and owned several organizations, while Bill got into the habit of abusing drugs and finally died of an overdose.

Stay by your teen's side through tough times so that if he makes a bad decision during his adolescence, it does not affect his adult life badly. This is not the same as being permissive or enforcing no consequences for errant behavior. Parents can deliver consequences while still being supportive.

ENCOURAGE INDEPENDENCE

Encouraging independence in children may sound simple, but it is actually not. It is more difficult than you think because independence involves decisions, actions, settlements, agreements, and all other aspects that are a part of an adult's life. Parents just get used to making all decisions for their kids like religion, neighborhood, social circles, and school. Things seem to be working fine and smooth, and then children hit adolescence and everything starts changing. Teens no longer appreciate the decisions made by their parents and they have a different opinion in almost everything.

This is part of their natural growth, but for parents, it is an entirely different situation. On the one hand, they feel offended because they face rejection for everything sane and logical they suggest to their teens; on the other hand, they sense that their kids are growing and they need to be independent in their life and decisions. What should be done?

ReachOut, a leading online mental health organization for young people and their parents in Australia, published an article titled "Teach Your Teenager Independence for the Future." The article highlighted that part of helping teens is to help them become independent. This involves agreeing on boundaries around their behavior so that both parent and child know what is expected and allowed. This then enables the child to have the opportunity to explore and discover things for themselves while also feeling safe and cared for.

ReachOut highlighted that boundaries will be different for each situation and should evolve as the teenager grows older. Here are some areas where boundaries can be useful:

- Going out with friends — where they can go and how late they can stay out.
- Contacting you while they are out — when and how often they should check in.
- Using social media and devices — what platforms are okay, and any device-free times.

This is like a transforming stage for the parents when they need to shift from the role of making decisions to sharing decisions and accepting rejections. Building independence in adolescence is important at this stage. Teens are growing in their mind and body. Their interests are changing. They are developing new values, goals, and thoughts.

Now, parents need to see this growing stage and its requirements from a more complete angle. It is not only their responsibility now to encourage independence but it is also a need for a teen to grow strong and become self-confident and independent in making decisions. Also, the teens are developing their self-identity as well as strengthening their connectedness to their parents. This connection is highly important. Patience plays a critical part in maintaining this connectedness.

Parents should respect their teen's individual identity and keep supporting and encouraging him or her throughout this adolescence period. There are several things that teens unintentionally pick up from their parents at this stage if their relation is filled with understanding, support, love, and encouragement. So, at a time when they are learning to make decisions on their own, they keep on tweaking them under the support of their parents. Hence, they will be developing their individual identity in the same environment that they grew up in.

Parents may find several choices of their teens confusing. It is quite possible that parents find their teens voting for Republicans while they supported Democrats all their lives — akin to voting for The Workers' Party while having supported The People's Action Party all their lives.

They may also find their high-scoring child in a close friendship with a secondary school or junior college dropout. However, parents need not freak out at these confusing behaviors or decisions of their teens, neither should they make these into big issues. In fact, these are little decisions which are a result of their temporary thinking and not deep logical decisions. Hence, no need to worry about these matters. Instead, it is more important that you let your teens feel that you are supportive and care for them honestly.

There are several advantages to parental support and encouragement. In a family environment where parents encourage open discussion and encourage their teens to think independently, parents and adolescents learn to trust each other. It requires a bit of trial and error on both sides, but with parental guidance the child can grow and learn, and go on to great things.

TOWARD MORE FREEDOM

Chris Hudson from UT: Understanding Teenagers offered a substantial amount of resources for parents online to engage teenagers. Based in Australia, the educator, father, husband, and youth worker with more than a decade of experience provided some insights into the freedom teenagers often gripe about and sometimes demands.

Parents often ask how much freedom they should give their teenager. How do I balance between my teenager's need for independence and ensuring their safety and well-being? How much is too much when it comes to giving teens responsibility? What is the right age to let my teenager do whatever activity even if it stresses me?

These are questions all parents of teenagers ask in one way or another at some point in their child's development. As with so many questions in life, there is no one right answer that can be simply rolled out for mass consumption. Each kid is unique and every family situation is different, so one simple answer that suits everyone is not possible.

There is no risk-free way of making these decisions. No 100% failure-proof method. Parents will always feel an element of fear in the process of letting go of their kids. But, to use an unattributed quote, at some point, we all need to "feel the fear and do it anyway!"

However, despite the lack of guarantees, in his article "When to Give Your Teenager More Freedom," Hudson wrote that there are some pretty solid principles that can definitely help make decisions about freedom, boundaries, and responsibility a lot easier (and less scary):

"Giving teens their freedom is their right."
"Parents need to start small."

When the kids hit the age of adolescence, parents start giving them freedom step by step. For example, give them the freedom to go with you to the mall but take a separate way and choose a few things on their own to purchase.

Appreciate their choices as much as possible. If they choose a different brand of soap that you have never used before, do not reject their choice though you can explain the reasons why you use the brand of soap that you usually buy.

If you find your teen is behaving overall fine at the mall, send him or her alone next time. Give him the freedom to choose the time or the brands of the items that he can buy. Also, leave your teen alone for an evening at home while you go out shopping or to meet friends. If the teen at home behaves well and acts as a responsible family member, leave him alone at home for a longer time next weekend. You will soon find that your teens appreciate the fact that you trust them. They also feel proud of being trusted.

So, if you are a parent and ready to start giving freedom to your teens but are not sure when and how to let your teenager take on some responsibilities or freedom, maybe you may want to consider this suggestion.

Step back for a minute and consider what your launch sequence is before engaging your teenager. Consider the following questions:

- "How old/mature are they?"
- "How many years /months to go until they are considered an adult?"
- "What skills/attitudes/values do they need to strengthen and develop?"
- "What can I do to aid their development?"
- "What expectations or lack of expectations do I have that is holding them back?"

With these things in mind, plot out the possible path for the immediate future. Then, take action on the next most important thing for your teenager.

DEVELOP TRUST

From wehavekids.com, a website created by moms, dads, educators, and family experts to share their unique expertise and knowledge about pregnancy, childbirth, parenting, and family life, an author Kendall Crane wrote that as kids get older they want to have more and more autonomy. They want to pursue their interests and make their own decisions. This can be scary for parents because there is just so much that could go wrong!

If you have built a strong foundation of trust from the beginning, then your kids know they can count on you, that you are on their side, they have had lots of practice with problem-solving, and are probably going to be able to make a lot of choices securely on their own. It will be easier to continue supporting, empathizing, responding, listening, and problem-solving if you have this foundation.

Many families do not have this foundation. It is not too late to start! It is, however, not always easy and smooth to start later on, but it is possible! When we first start to prioritize trust in our relationship after years of parents demonstrating other parenting priorities, kids will do a lot of testing. Try to remember that they aren't pushing boundaries, they are testing the love and trust. It can be quite intense, but if you stick with it, the dust will settle over time and you will see a transformation in your relationship with your kids.

A few tips to get you started:

1. Remember that your kids are always doing their best in every situation with the tools they have. The best way to gain our kid's trust is to give it, especially in difficult moments.
2. Remember that behavior is communication. If you can't figure out what is going on, talk to your kids and be ready to listen and not lecture.
3. Validation and empathy are your best friends when building a relationship of trust with your older kids. Their experience is just as valid as that of any other person, even if we don't understand that experience.

Trust is a mutual feeling and develops with mutual work. Parents who encourage their teens to talk and share their feelings automatically trust them. And, when the parents trust their teens, the teens feel great about themselves and also about their parents. Studies show that teens decide to share their thoughts and activities with their parents, but it is basically the parents' positive behavior and reassurance that encourage the teens to share and talk.

Adolescents long to be trusted, especially when they feel that they are not doing anything really wrong. Parents should start showing their trust in their teens. They can be vigilant of their activities and decisions. But, there is a difference in being vigilant and showing distrust. Parental distrust can be damaging. If the parents read the diary of their teens, search their cupboards, read their emails, monitor their use of the computer secretly, and check on their activities outside by asking accompanying teens or the school admin, they break a huge structure of trust for them in the hearts of their teens. When parents show their distrust in their teens without any proper reason, they suffer the consequences heavily. Their relationship with their teens is shaken and the mutual respect is badly damaged.

Teens interpret this distrust as their parents thinking of them as bad kids. This is a misunderstanding that has no solution because the kids do not simply go and ask their parents, "do you think we are bad?" Even if they do so, parents are never going to say, "We are just suspicious of what you are doing."

The misunderstanding damages mutual love and trust. So, do not let the unknown and baseless fear in your hearts lead you to get involved in things that show distrust. There are other real issues that you should be more concerned about rather than checking your teen's mail or cupboards. You need to be smart in maintaining a balance between your surveillance and trust. Never let surveillance become an act of trust!

MONITORING

Many parents misunderstand monitoring. So, first, understand what it means to monitor your teens. Monitoring means having knowledge of your teens. It means knowing where your teen is at 10.00 p.m. Successful parenting means closeness to your children. This means staying aware of what they like, where they go, and what they do, not in a treacherous manner, but with love and honesty, openly and not discretely, in a friendly manner and not formally.

What are the advantages of monitoring? Many parents think that monitoring means knowing everything about the teens' life to criticize, correct, direct, and command on what to do and what not to do. This is the completely wrong meaning of monitoring and this is not the purpose of monitoring. Basically, teens are reluctant to share their personal details with parents and let them know what they do and where they go. When they find that the result of sharing with parents means getting criticism and restrictions, they stop sharing anything. That would be a complete failure of your parenting.

Monitoring means your mature and logical closeness and presence close to the teens' brain. Hence, the teens get the benefit of your wisdom. This does not even remotely mean that you impose your wisdom on them by force. So, monitoring is keeping track of your children while there is the warmth of friendliness, care, and sharing between you and them.

When parents monitor their teens, they maintain a genuine interest in their teens' life and interests. They also care about their friends and the people they hang out with.

Monitoring teens is not an easy job. Sometimes, teens do not bother to communicate. Other times, parents are busy. Often, job responsibilities, home management, and other responsibilities make it quite complicated to monitor teens. However, it is the benefit of monitoring that makes it worth the effort.

There are fewer chances that teens get into trouble when they are sure that parents are aware of everything. It is the feeling of being monitored that keeps them safe from several crazy choices. So, monitored teens are less likely to steal, do drug, cheat, lie, or engage in sexual behavior.

Parents must learn the following points to be good monitors for their teens:

- who your teen is with,
- where your teen is going,

- what your teen plans to do,
- when your teen will be home.

Do not ask these questions like you are interrogating, but while conversing and talking, collect all the necessary information. So, stay in touch with your teens. Make it clear to your teens that they should give you a call when they are going to be late back home. You can also call them when they are late.

Set an example of informing the family members at home when you are late. Make a call and let the teens at home know that you will be late.

Monitoring teens' activities and interests alone is not enough. Keep monitoring their thoughts as well. Do not try to control their thoughts. Controlling his or her thoughts will not specifically control his or her actions. Monitoring the thoughts keeps you aware of what your teen is going to do or what views he is growing with.

Parents wonder what the purpose of monitoring is when they cannot try to change the wrong views that are developing in the mind of their teen. The answer to this is simple.

Have an overall good communication with your teens. Have talks and conversations regularly. Introduce them to the values and views that you want them to understand. Be open about the focal points of your concerns. Also, make sure that there are strong bonds of love between you and your teens. In fact, it is a part of the human psyche to listen to the views of someone you love. So, if you love your teens and care for them, they absolutely would love to listen to your thoughts and appreciate your values. The influence of love is strong. Exploit this influence because it is long-lasting and deeply penetrating.

Another good solution to monitor your teens is to let your teens get involved in activities and sports that are supervised by adults, like taking tennis lessons or joining a club, so that they remain in close vicinity to adult brains. Welcome your teens' friends at home. No matter how loud or disturbing they are, you have an excellent opportunity to monitor them. But, do not stay around all the time and make them feel as if they are living with an FBI agent. Give the kids their space. After all, you are not dealing with criminals.

HAVE FUN TOGETHER

Have plenty of fun with your teens whenever you get an opportunity. Go shopping together, talk and crack jokes the whole way while shopping. Try a sweater, a pair of goggles, a pair of new slippers, etc. Or, go to watch a movie together.

Do not reject every fun-filled opportunity because you are too busy. If you do not have time to find out how to have fun with your teens, put their interests first. Choose a place of their choice to go to play some sports, swim for a while, watch a movie, or go to an amusement park — somewhere he or she is going to enjoy. But, do not get dragged by them each time they want you to go somewhere. Teens need to accept your choices sometimes as you accept their choices sometimes.

Family vacations are a great time for every family member, including teens. You can have plenty of fun in many different ways during such vacations. Moreover, these vacations are not meant to involve any scoldings, strict timings, scheduled activities, etc. So, the teens have a fun time of their liking. They feel happy and fulfilled by the pleasant hours they spend in an utterly family atmosphere.

WARNING: Never find an opportunity to start a discussion on a sensitive topic like their school performance or their choice of friends on such an outing. The teens will quickly assume that going out means tricking them into boring and embarrassing discussions. They would not like to go out with you anymore because no one likes to be caught by surprise in an unwanted situation.

COACHING ON COPING SKILLS

Life is not a smooth journey where everything is black and white. There are several shades of colors that come in between white and black and your teens need your coaching to learn how to cope with the changing situations.

If your teens do not learn coping skills during their growing and developing age, they may get lost at many points in their lives and turn to drugs and alcohol to cope with difficult situations. It will be very difficult for them to learn how to deal alone.

Even learning different strategies to cope with the ups and downs of life will be almost impossible for them. This is the most straightforward way to make it easy and comprehensible.

For example, when you are depressed, say loudly to your family, "I feel like I am drowning, so I think I should go out and breathe in ample fresh air to refresh my head."

Here, you are setting an example of coping with depression. Your teens will absorb your strategy and feel that when they feel stressed or depressed they should become active and get some exercise. Hence, they will be able to cope with their own moments of disaster when they arise.

Here are a few coping skills that can really work for your teens:

- Avoid stressful relationships.
- Spend time with family and friends.
- Talk to someone about your feelings (i.e., family, friend, or counselor).
- Don't watch the news for a month.
- Exercise.
- Write in a journal.
- Join an extracurricular activity.
- Read books or magazines that make you feel good.
- Volunteer.

These are just a few examples. You can be innovative and find several more coping skills with a little search depending on your lifestyle, culture, social status, interests, and even family size.

HARD FACTS

The following are some hard facts about teens' development and psychological structure. They are informed by science. Some may sound discriminatory and even condescending, but that is not the point. These are all about natural effects. These facts happen due to nature that carries habits and traits from one person to another. We can even say that these facts are unavoidable purely because we interact with each other. Parents interact with their children, adults with each other. As such, we influence each other, verbally and non-verbally; regardless, whether we know it or not:

- What will be the future of the kids or how much education they receive depends on the education level of the mother.
- Women who spent their youth in unrestrained behavior have little to no trust in their own teenagers.
- Teenage girls show a similar attitude to sex and drugs as their mother even if their mother does not talk about the subject.
- Parents give their kids the motivation to achieve academic success or excel in other things.
- Students who have strong and close bonds with their parents are less likely to drop out of school.
- Families who enjoy at least five meals together a week have kids who are more motivated to succeed and less likely to engage in drugs.

These things seem so simple and like a normal routine of life that we do not even notice that they can have such a deep impact on teens. But, studies over years on countless teens have proven these simple things of life as hard facts.

Teenagers are much smarter than adults.

Moreover, teens do not have much life experience. But, they believe that they are smarter and cleverer than their parents.

That is why it is difficult to convince them about anything, and this is the reason why they do not feel like sharing their feelings many times.

Often you hear from them that you are too old to understand them. This hurts, but you should know that your teen is just developing a prefrontal side and he does not really mean it when he says so. In fact, it is his feelings, which are developing fast and transforming, which tell him now that he is more aware of many things than you are.

Once the teens are in the higher stage of brain development, they realize that things are different from what they used to assume. Their logical part starts becoming stronger and they think more rather than just feel.

Now, this is an important stage of life for them. If they have experienced too much criticism from you or lecturing, it will be difficult for them to confess their past mistakes and repair their relationship with you.

So, the strong point here is that you keep your behavior as caring and forgiving as possible. Give your teens time to get back to you based on their own logic, and your past good dealing and wise handling of matters would help them repair what they damaged because of their emotional state.

SUMMARY

There are effective strategies in engaging with youth.

1. Keeping communication open with the youth.
   a. Being physically present and available for them to confide in you.
   b. Having non-directive, open conversations on the youth's topics of interest, while listening with interest and quiet approval.
2. Being supportive and encouraging to the youth, even in the face of bad decisions.

3. Encouraging independence by sharing decision-making processes and accepting rejections.
    a. Setting boundaries to manage expectations from both parties.
4. Working toward giving the youth more freedom.
    a. Parents should start small and give it step by step.
5. Developing trust in the relationship.
    a. Parents earn the youth's trust when they first give it.
    b. Excessive surveillance causes distrust.
6. Monitoring and having knowledge of the youth.
    a. Obtaining information in genuine interest and a non-interrogative manner.
        i. Whereabouts
        ii. Social groups
        iii. Plans
        iv. Personal thoughts
7. Engaging in fun-filled opportunities and activities with the youth.
    a. Such interactions should avoid discussions of sensitive topics.
8. Helping the youth develop healthy coping strategies.
    a. Parents should live out said strategies for the youth to emulate.

Youth instinctively assume they are smarter than their parents, which results in a difficulty in convincing them to share their feelings. They will eventually realize their erroneous ways as they grow. It is critical for parents to maintain a caring and forgiving relationship, which makes it easier for them to confess past mistakes and commit toward positive change.

Chapter 13

Five Things to Avoid

There are knowingly or unknowingly some things that should be avoided by parents with regard to their teens. This is because these can damage teens' brain development, cause them to feel lost, and fail. Unfortunately, parents think that these things are helpful and can work strongly in favor of teens' training to become strong and guided adolescents.

NEGATIVE EXPECTATIONS

"I know you will do drugs!" "Since the day you were born, I never felt that you will be up to any good."

Sentences like these and many others showing clear negative expectations of parents are extremely destructive for teens.

Parents think they are letting the teens know that they are aware of their habits and they cannot do anything behind the backs of their parents. In the hope to sensitise their teens to "watch what they do", otherwise, they can be caught in the act by their parents and be served a punishment; parents don't realise they are setting themselves up for failurel, they forget that they are destroying their own kids.

The fear of the teens going off-track is there in the hearts of every parent. There is a big world outside with all the options open for their teens who are new to everything. Their reasoning is poor and their logic is incomplete. They may choose wrong; they may go beyond the point of no return. These fears are inevitable.

But, parents need to understand that teens rarely pick gangs and drugs when they have great family bonds and they enjoy honest family love and care.

Also, teens who have the opportunity to talk and discuss their feelings and issues with their parents do not opt for drugs, gangs and sex. Again, it falls on parents to encourage their child to open up and share his feelings. Kids are often reluctant to share their thoughts. They are not bold enough to state the details of their nightmares and daydreams, especially to their parents.

Using phrases that show negative expectations never helps teens. They never think, "Oh, damn, that is going to be bad! Let me not do the drugs!"

They develop an obstinate desire to do what they wish.

Showing negative expectations cuts the cords of love between parents and their teens.

So, discard any self-serving expectations and let go of your desire to feel good by saying the most unpleasant and toxic phrases to your teens. Instead, stay AFFIRMING and POSITIVE.

There is no end to good expectations. Why not make the best use of them? There is no lack of love in your heart for your kids. Why not make it obvious to them?

If you focus on the positive and good side of life, your teen will have no time and not even one single thought about going to the bad options.

Esther Entin, MD, from *The Doctors Will See You Now*, wrote about how "Expectations Can Hurt Teens":

> "The researchers, Christy M. Buchanan of Wake Forest University and Johna L. Hughes of the University of North Carolina, Chapel Hill, predicted that when mothers and adolescents had negative expectations for future behavior during adolescence, the adolescent behavior one year later would indeed be characterized by more rebelliousness, risk-taking, and alienation.
>
> They expected this would be true even when established predictors of adolescent behavior were taken into account. The interviewed participants and collected information from questionnaires when the students were in sixth grade and a year later when they were in seventh. They assessed risk taking/rebelliousness, susceptibility to peer influence, quality of the parent-adolescent relationship, and degree of parental control. They found that when mothers expected their teens to engage in stereotypical risk-taking, rebellious and alienated behaviors, their child's later adolescent behavior indeed showed these qualities."

Sharon Holbrook echoed the same sentiments and wrote the following in *Your Teen* in the article "Don't Expect the Worst from Teens — Or You Just Might Get It":

> "Christy Buchanan, professor of psychology at Wake Forest University, has studied this phenomenon for years and found that parents' expectations of risky behavior can lead to higher engagement in risk-taking behaviors like experimentation with alcohol, drugs, and sex. Similarly, expecting teenage years

to be a time of emotionally charged "storm and stress" makes it more likely that the teen years will be just that."

Simply put, do not buy into the stereotypes!

Psychologist John Duffy, the author of *The Available Parent* and host of the new podcast Undue Anxiety, agrees. He said, "When parents lower their bar of expectations for their children, kids will recognize that as a show of no-confidence in them."

Plus, it is exhausting for teenagers to hear only the negative — what you are currently doing wrong, or what you will eventually do wrong. Buchanan reminds parents to not just to have high expectations but also to focus on the positive things kids are already doing, such as managing schedules packed with school, homework, activities, and chores. "How often do we give them a really hearty pat on the back?" she asks.

SMALL ISSUES. BIG FUSS

"Why did you choose this haircut?"
"This red dress is not for this evening's outing!"
"Do not buy these sandals. The neighbor's girl was wearing them and they looked ugly."

Before you start poking your teen with these small details of life, think of the big picture. Ask yourself the following questions:

- Does his choice of hair cut really look to be a "mistake?"
- What if she wears this red dress? After all, she is trying to enjoy her choice and the evening event.
- If the sandals looked ugly on neighbor's girl, they should not necessarily look ugly on my daughter, too.

Parents make quite a fuss on small points which are just a matter of choice for teens. They have no bad impact on their upbringing. But, the freedom of choice in these small matters gives the teens an opportunity to practice their decision-making powers.

Parents want their teens to be exactly what they imagine them to be. Instead of trying to accept their teens' choice open-heartedly, they criticize, object, and frown upon them frequently. They think that they are helping their teen look smart and good.

This is a poor thought and improper behavior which never leads to what they imagine as "smarter" kids.

By interfering in small choices, the parents snatch away from their teens the opportunity to experiment with new things and learn from their own actions.

In his book *Don't Sweat the Small Stuff* and *It's All Small Stuff: Simple Ways to Keep the Little Things from Taking Over Your Life* (Don't Sweat the Small Stuff Series), Richard Carlson wrote the following:

> "Often we allow ourselves to get all worked up about things that, upon closer examination, aren't really that big a deal. We focus on little problems and concerns and blow them way out of proportion. A stranger, for example, might cut in front of us in traffic. Rather than let it go, and go on with our day, we convince ourselves that we are justified in our anger. We play out an imaginary confrontation in our mind. Many of us might even tell someone else about the incident later on rather than simply let it go."

TOO MUCH INDEPENDENCE

Giving teens the freedom of action without limits can be dangerous. Teens do not have much experience of life and their PFC is still at the developing stage. At a time when it is encouraged to let the teens decide what they want and what they need, parents need to maintain limits to their freedom.

Giving too much freedom at an early age can push the teen into negative behavior. They can choose things which are risky and can harm them.

Jen Klein is a New England-based technical writer for SheKnows and a mother of three. SheKnows.com is a progressive, inclusive space for women to find the practical information they need and the daily inspiration they want to live full, authentic lives. Jen wrote the following:

> "There's no absolute formula for granting teen independence. Lucky for everyone, independence is a process. It does not happen all at once but rather builds over time. The kind of independence you grant your 14-year-old is not the same as what you grant your 17-year-old — but hopefully the independence you grant at 14 will help build a foundation for what happens at 17.
>
> There are lots of things a teenager can do. Everything from just plain spending time alone or with friends, to taking on a part-time job, to taking responsibility for more chores at home and beyond.
>
> Some of it you may have taken for granted! But all of these are part of building independence and trust in your child so that

when it does come time for your little (big!) bird to fly the nest, you will both be confident that he or she will do so confidently and successfully. Start by granting a little more freedom — a little later curfew, a little more trust — as time passes (and with appropriate checks and balances). Before you know it, you will have a confident, trustworthy young adult in your household — even as you miss the tiny baby he once was.

As with every age and stage, not every teen is ready for certain responsibilities or levels of independence at that same age. For some, it's appropriate to hold back — and for some, a little push is okay. Your daughter, for example, might not like the idea of a week away from you on a church mission trip even if she loves the idea and is committed to her youth group. It's likely okay to give her a little push and insist she goes. She'd be in a well-organized group with a safety net, after all. It is a risk for both of you — and hopefully, one that will end with your daughter saying, "Mom, you were right. I can be away and be okay. I can use a hammer and build things. I can do a lot of things."

Christine Carter wrote the following in the article "How Independent Should Teenagers Be?" on *Psychology Today*:

"The answer (relating to giving freedom), according to neuropsychologist William Stixrud and teen coach Ned Johnson, authors of The Self-Driven Child, is to hand the decision-making reins over to our teens. You read that right: By adolescence, we parents need to (take a deep breath and) let them make their own decisions about their lives."

As a sociologist and author of *The New Adolescence, The Sweet Spot* and *Raising Happiness*, Carter is also a senior fellow at University of California, Berkeley's Greater Good Science

Center. She draws on scientific research to help people lead their most courageous, joyful, meaningful, and productive lives. She further highlighted that the following:

> "Letting our teens become the decision-makers does not mean that we become permissive, indulgent, or disengaged parents. Fifty years of research has consistently shown that "authoritative" parenting is good for teens' health and well-being. Authoritative parents set and consistently enforce clear limits, and they are warm and engaged in their kids' lives. Authoritative parenting helps kids develop self-control — making them less likely to have problems with drugs, alcohol, or teen pregnancy. Teenagers with authoritative parents do better in school, have greater self-confidence, and have more friends."

Raising Independent Teenagers: Ideas

The Australian Parenting Website (raisingchildren.net.au) highlighted that achieving independence is an essential part of a child's journey to adulthood. Therefore, to make this journey successfully, children need freedom to try new things. But, they still need parental guidance and support. Here, are some proposals to help parent and child find the right balance.

Show your child lots of love and support

Your love and support are essential for your child's self-esteem. Young people who feel good about themselves often have more confidence to discover who they are and what they want to do with their lives.

Your child might not always want physical affection from you. But, you can show your love and support by doing the following:

1. staking a genuine interest in your child's interests, hobbies, and friends,
2. making time to listen when your child needs to talk,
3. giving your child space and privacy,
4. regularly saying "I love you."

Respect your child's feelings and opinions

Try to tune into your child's feelings. It might help you to remember that your child could be confused and upset by the physical, social, and emotional changes of adolescence. Your child needs your emotional guidance and stability during this time.

Taking your child's opinions and ideas seriously gives an important boost to her self-esteem. Your child's opinions might be different from yours and more like those of her peers. This might be hard to handle, but exploring opinions and ideas is one of the ways your child works out where she fits in the world. And, if you have a difference of opinion, it is a good chance for you to talk about how people often have different perspectives and that is OKAY.

Talking about your own opinions and feelings calmly can help keep the lines of communication open and model positive ways of relating to others.

Establish clear and fair family rules

Clear family rules about behavior, communication, and socializing will help your child understand where the limits are and what you expect. Rules will also help you be consistent in how you treat your child. Once the rules are in place, apply them consistently.

Your family rules are likely to change as your child develops. As children get more mature, they can make a bigger contribution to the rules and the consequences for breaking them. Involving your child in developing rules helps him understand the principles behind them. Every family has different rules. You can talk with your child about this and explain that his friends might have different rules or a different number of rules.

If you set the limits too strictly, your child might not have enough room to grow and try new experiences. This period is a learning curve for both of you. Be prepared for some trial and error.

Treat your child in a way that's appropriate for her stage

Younger teenagers might think they are ready to make their own decisions, but they often have not developed the decision-making skills they need to handle significant responsibility without your help. It can be a good idea to explain to your younger child why younger and older children are given different amounts and types of responsibilities.

It is likely that the independence your child wants — and the amount of independence you want to give — will change as your child goes through the teenage years. Be prepared to adjust and keep negotiating as you move together along the learning curve.

Help your child develop decision-making skills

When your child needs to make a decision, a problem-solving approach can help her develop independent decision-making skills. This involves the following:

- finding out about different options,
- talking about the pros and cons of different actions,
- weighing up the pros and cons to make the best decision,
- brainstorming what to do if things don't go according to plan,
- giving your child feedback on how she handles the process.

You can also include your child in family decision-making. This is another chance to boost your child's self-esteem and show that you value his input.

When it comes to big decisions that affect your child, try to make those decisions with your child, not for her. These might be decisions about school, further study, staying out late, and so on.

Your teenager's brain continues to mature into the early twenties. In particular, the decision-making part of the brain is still developing and your child is still learning to control impulses. Teenagers, especially younger teenagers, might be less capable of understanding the consequences of their behavior.

Provide safe opportunities for your child to exercise independence

Activities that are safe and supported but that give your child freedom and time away from you can help your child to the following:

- learn new skills and test new abilities,
- take positive risks,
- foster a sense of belonging,
- build resilience.

For example, there might be a youth group or sports club in your area that your child would like to be involved in. When your child is old enough, a part-time job is a great way for him to develop independence.

SPENDING LESS TIME WITH TEENS

Many parents limit the time that they spend with their teens either because of their busy life or the realization that their kids have grown up. They need their own space, their own time, and parents leave them on their own most of the times and do not spend a few healthy hours with them.

The reality is that adolescents need as much of their parents' time as younger kids do, but in a slightly different form. It is not their physical needs that require parental care, but now it is their life in a broader sense, for example, they have confusion and questions that need a discussion with an adult.

Parents who leave their teens alone to their own devices in these years of life commit a big mistake. The problem is that teens do not bother their parents for help in finding answers to their questions. They are just happy with the fact that they enjoy more freedom and stay busy for several hours away from home.

Leaving adolescents on their own is not a good parenting tool, and does it not bring positive results either. Secure Teen, an Australia-based company providing parental control services for smartphones for parents of children between the ages of 7 and 17, pointed out the following:

> "Parents need to understand that no matter how much money they spend on their teens, the risk of spending less time with

children is just too high. The time you spend with your child is something that cannot be compensated. Time parents spend with children is important and there's no replacement for it. This can even turn your child into a spoiled brat."

Jennifer Brozak, a freelance writer, blogger, and photographer, wrote the following on *Hello Motherhood* (www.hellomotherhood.com):

"It is no secret that communicating with your children is important. In fact, according to the U.S. Department of Health and Human Services, the simple art of listening to your child is one of the most basic, but most effective, ways to prevent your child from engaging in risky behavior. Moreover, reports from the Office of National Drug Control Strategy indicate that strong family bonds can prevent children from developing drug problems. Whether he is 2 or 12 years of age, if you feel that you are not spending enough one-on-one time bonding with your child, try enhancing the time that you do have by simply talking and listening to him when you are cooking, eating dinner, shopping or driving.

According to research reported on familyfacts.org, the children of parents who are frequently absent throughout the day — such as when they wake up, come home from school, eat dinner and go to bed — are more likely to feel emotionally distressed than their peers. In addition, familyfacts.org reports that there is a strong correlation between parental involvement and a child's self-esteem and "internal controls", which points to a child's ability to regulate his emotions. In other words, involved parents equate to happier kids.

Not spending enough time with your child can lead to a multitude of detrimental behavioral problems. For instance, according to research reported on familyfacts.org, children who do not have strong bonds with their parents are more likely to become involved in risky, antisocial behaviors, including aggression and delinquency, unsafe sexual relationships and teen pregnancy and tobacco and illegal drug use. Many of these behaviors can be prevented through the simple act of spending time with your child."

There are a number of colorful activities and games that you can enjoy together with your teens. Kids always enjoy the company of their parents, especially when there are common interests like going fishing, hiking, or playing sports together. Mothers can find several opportunities at home when they can let their teen girls join them, for example, cooking, crafting, and home decorating. Apart from these activities, simply eat dinner together as a family. If you have dinner together every day, you can talk, discuss, and offer suggestions at dinner time.

PROVISIONING TEENS WITH EXTRA STUFF

Most parents think that the success and happiness of their children involves owning more clothes, shoes, toys, a luxurious home setting, and a large amount of pocket money. They presume that a well-provided kid is able to cope with life in a better way. He gains confidence and feels stronger among his peers. Hence, they provide them with everything the kids ask for even more.

They tend to forget that owning more and unnecessarily can deprive them of some classic personality traits that are helpful throughout their life like patience, selflessness, and sacrifice.

Providing a child with whatever she asks for spoils her. There are several negative effects of becoming a spoiled child and it is very difficult to correct the damage done to the personality of the child after she grows into an adult.

Fredric Neuman, MD, author of "Come One, Come All," wrote an article in *Psychology Today* about "Spoiling a Child. And not spoiling a child. The difference will have a considerable effect":

> "The problem with being a "spoiled adult" goes far beyond the fact that such an individual, demanding much of the time, is likely to seem unpleasant, even obnoxious, to the people around him. A spoiled person is unhappy. He feels frustrated, even cheated, if he or she is not allowed to indulge his or her wishes immediately.
>
> Being spoiled suggests to most people a desire for more and more possessions, and that is indeed one aspect of being spoiled, but another is an unwillingness to conform to ordinary social expectations. Somebody who won't do what he or she is expected to do is spoiled. That person may seem disgruntled, complaining, resentful, and self-centered. Such a person is preoccupied with thoughts of what he or she does not have. And lacking discipline, that person may fail at work and in social situations."

Considering possessions a means for growth is a wrong idea in the minds of many parents. If owning a lot of stuff meant success and achievement, Thomas Edison and Colonel Sanders, for example, would not have achieved the everlasting success that they did. Happiness, success, and a sense of pride are true feelings which do not depend on possessing material items. These true feelings come from true hard work, determination, and patience.

Giving the teens what they want spoils them. They grow up wanting everything to come their way without any effort. They spend heartlessly; they demand heedlessly. Over-provisioning the teens with stuff they do not really need changes their perception of life and work. A time of their life which should be the foundation for a successful adult life becomes full of material desires.

Give your child your company, your love, your care, and your guidance toward a happy future. These are the greatest luxuries you provide your teens with!

SUMMARY

Despite having good intentions, parents often react in negative ways toward their youth, which serves to damage the relationship and set them up for failure. There are five negative behaviors that are prevalent:

1. Having negative expectations of the youth.
2. Creating a big fuss over small issues.
3. Providing too much independence. The following are guidelines to developing independent youth:
   a. Showing lots of love and support.
   b. Respecting their feelings and opinions.
   c. Establishing clear and fair family rules.
   d. Treating them in an age-appropriate manner.
   e. Helping them develop decision-making skills.
   f. Providing safe opportunities to exercise independence.
4. Spending less time with their children.
5. Provisioning youth with extra stuff.

Chapter 14

The Challenges and Beyond

We have almost come to the end of our learning journey here, and before we wrap it up, we want to acknowledge that when we define adolescence as a period of immense changes and challenges, we need to admit the fact that each challenge has several different forms and types. If one teen faces a challenge in a certain form, the other may not face it in the same way or with the same intensity. One teen might be bold and excited to go through a challenge, while the other might be terrified.

WHAT MAKES THE CHALLENGES ALWAYS DIFFERENT AMONG ADOLESCENTS?

Growing Up Environment

There are several reasons that are the direct reason why adolescents face challenges differently among themselves. One common factor is that the physical conditions are different in every individual. Some children face certain physical disorders or face an accident during the early years of their life which affects their personality in some cases and mostly affects the way their body grows and the hormonal changes that take place.

The way the children grow and the responses they get from their parents also make their challenges different from that of other adolescents. For example, a father who is a caring and sharing father throughout the childhood of his daughter makes it easy for her to ask questions and discuss her issues at school with him. This makes her challenges a lot easier and less intimidating.

If you see the behavior of such a child who grew under caring and sharing parents and the behavior of another teen at school whose father was extremely strict and harsh, you might think that the two teens are different because of their personal approach toward life at school. Meanwhile, the real reason is parental care and relation.

Cultural Boundaries

Cultural boundaries and family status also affect the way a child suffers from the challenges he faces. Adolescents could feel that their challenges have become enormous because of certain conditions surrounding them, for example, a foster family, legal or illegal migration, and jobless parents. Kids of such families feel their challenges in a different way and, subsequently, respond to them differently.

UNICEF reported on migration and children in the following way:

> "Migration presents both opportunities and challenges for societies, communities, and individuals. Migration alters the structure of families. While it is true that economic factors are major drivers, migration involves highly diverse groups of people, including girls, boys, women, men, and better-off as well as poorer people.

Experience has shown that children are affected by migration in different ways: children are left behind by migrant parents; they are brought along with their migrating parents; and they migrate alone, independently of parents and adult guardians. Other children do not move but are nevertheless affected because they live in communities that send or receive large numbers of migrants. Some children are return migrants or have been repatriated.

So, you can see that family situations can increase the challenges of teens, intensify them, make them more difficult or complicated, etc."

THREE-DIMENSIONAL CHALLENGES

The challenges that adolescents face are effectively three dimensional. The Counselling Connection Website hosted by the Australian Institute of Professional Counsellors (AIPC) provides us with some insights into the three dimensions. We need to know these dimensions to understand what our teens face and how we should behave as parents to keep our behavior amicable and friendly with our youth.

Biological Challenges

Adolescence starts with a very prominent event which is well defined and everyone knows it — puberty. This event is all about biological changes. These changes occur due to the start of new systems in the body and the release of hormones which had not been there while a kid was a child. Of course, these hormonal changes can impact the relationship of teens with parents and siblings at home, with friends and peers in school, or with the community.

In his book *Brainstorm*, Dan Seigel explained these biological changes in the following explicit words:

> "Puberty is marked by the development of the body and its changes in secondary sexual characteristics (growing genitals and larger muscles in boys; widening hips and budding breasts in girls). This sexual maturation anatomically is associated with increases in chemicals that are distributed throughout the body, and hormones of various sorts that help regulate growth and activation of the sexual regions of the body. Changes in the brain itself may not correlate directly with the timing of these changes in the body, so we cannot state that mental changes necessarily go along with these sexual changes. However, the increase in circulating sex hormones following the onset of puberty creates new and intense sexual drives, feelings of attraction, and erotic arousal."

Cognitive Challenges

Jean Piaget, in his theory on social development, believed that adolescence is the time when young people develop cognitively from "concrete operations" to "formal operations." So, they are able to deal with ideas, concepts, and abstract theories. However, it takes time for confidence to build while using these newly acquired skills, and they may make mistakes in judgment. Learning through success and failure is part of the challenge in the learning process for the adolescents.

Some of the cognitive challenges include being egocentric, self-conscious, and imaginative. They often think of themselves as a celebrity and behave as if they were on stage performing. Hence, you find them in their room often singing or doing anything else that their favorite idols do like boxing, acting, and rapping.

Adolescents' minds are growing bigger and they are learning several different things in life whether they are skills, experiences, or mental calculations of events. This is a process of becoming an adult and being responsible in life.

Their thoughts that we think of as weird or improper are also a part of the process. They think that no one can understand them, their feelings are unique, they must keep their secrets away from everyone, etc.

The cognitive development is slow in teens as it completes at the later stages of adolescence. But, it continues throughout the adolescence absorbing different aspects of mental maturity. It includes values, care, caution, rationality, patience, practicality, taking decisions, etc.

How soon can an adolescent reach full mental maturity?

While we have already discussed this extensively in the earlier part of the book, I cited a very different source to reflect on another perspective.

NPR is an independent non-profit media organization that was founded on a mission to create a more informed public. Every day, NPR connects with millions of Americans on the air, online, and in person to explore the news, ideas, and what it means to be human. In the article "Brain Maturity Extends Well Beyond Teen Years," Sandra Aamodt, neuroscientist and co-author of the book *Welcome to Your Child's Brain: How the Mind Grows from Conception to College*, was quoted as saying the following:

"...the changes that happen between 18 and 25 are a continuation of the process that starts around puberty, and 18-year-olds are about halfway through that process. Their prefrontal cortex is not yet fully developed. That's the part of the brain that helps you to inhibit impulses and to plan and organize your behavior to reach a goal. And the other part of the brain that is different in adolescence is that the brain's reward system becomes highly active right around the time of puberty and then gradually goes back to an adult level, which it reaches around age 25 and that makes adolescents and young adults more interested in entering uncertain situations to seek out and try to find whether there might be a possibility of gaining something from those situations."

Psychological Challenges

There are several psychological challenges and some of them can be quite difficult to deal with. They start around the time of puberty and continue until the end of the mid-twenties or a little more.

When a boy is going through his teenage years, he is converting fully into an adult man. It is a life-changing process; more responsibilities are assigned to him. A certain behavior becomes a person's identity and many different adult expectations become a part of his life like accountability, care, commitment, and determination.

Psychological challenges at this stage of life are mostly related to the new things that occur in the life of adolescents. The boy cannot easily adjust to the changes and cannot easily meet all the challenges. Leaving home, for example, is a tough challenge. Dealing with this challenge single-handedly makes it more difficult.

The changes and efforts of adjusting can be anxiety provoking and extremely stressful. Therefore, adolescents have a decreased tolerance for most of the things that happen around them, especially the changes. Hence, they go through the double efforts of adjusting to the changes and handling their mood swings. The efforts of modulating their behavior are difficult for them and they need proper assistance in this age, not in the form of instructions and "dos and don'ts," but in the form of support, company, care, etc.

So, the adolescents face changes in their cognitive, biological, psychological, moral, spiritual, and social spheres. Dealing with these huge changes can be overwhelming. Their attitude changes and they suffer from unstable moods. That is why it is observed that family members suddenly feel like they have a stranger at home.

TOP FIVE MOST IMPORTANT CHALLENGES ADOLESCENTS FACE

Adolescents experience many different changes and challenges. Some of them are comparatively easier, while some others are huge and cause complex problems in teens. Since the big challenges influence the teens badly and affect them psychologically and physically, parents and teachers need to know several ways of supporting teens in facing these challenges. The teens who get enough support at home and school outgrow these challenges sooner than other teens who are not able to find enough support. They also do not suffer from the long-term effects of these challenges.

There are some adults who still struggle with some challenges that should have long finished, like overcoming social anxiety. Some adults face relationship issues like adolescents because they did not learn to handle this issue while they were still young.

Adolescents who are able to face their challenges more successfully grow as stronger adults who are able to face the challenges of their career, married life, social responsibilities, and future planning more successfully.

The quality of life and the level of enjoyment are noticeably higher in those adults who went through their teenage years with the strong support of parents and teachers.

Here are the five most important challenges that teens face and some ways in which parents and teachers can diminish their bad effects.

1. Changes in the Body

This is one of the giant challenges that needs immense effort from adolescents. The look of their skin changes. Acne appears on different parts of the face in particular; their bodies grow bigger and more muscular. The voice starts changing from the childish tone to a heavier adult tone. But, this change is gradual and until it completely changes, it goes through stages of unpleasant pitches. Often, teens do not feel comfortable with the changes in their voice.

Adolescents cannot accept the changes their bodies experience easily. This is all too much to feel comfortable with. The acne on their face, growing hair on their body, increased sweating, and larger body size make them feel clumsy and they behave awkwardly, which adds to their troubles. These changes are natural but how adolescents can feel normal with the process of growing older while all this happens to them is the real challenge. They struggle to get out of this discomfort by choosing different products to cure acne, remove the hair from their body, and make their appearance better. As it is really important for teens to look attractive, they do everything to get there. But, not every choice is right and harmless for them.

There are several ways that parents and teachers can help them. Mostly, the best tool comes in the form of talking. Again, we emphasize that this is not a talk that is filled with a lot of advice and suggestions. This is more about talking and discussing the options to clarify the difference between the different choices that teens can make.

Give them ample time to talk about their fears and troubles to you. When you show your concern and warmth, it will be easier for them to seek your help in choosing the best thing in several cases. The US department of education pointed out the following:

> "We know that certain things increase the chances that children will avoid major problems. Having warm, supportive parents who also draw clear rules and monitor sufficiently is key. In addition, a child with an easy-going temperament, good social skills and a sense of humor is generally able to deal with problems. A child who attends school and lives in a neighborhood that provides many supports is also, on average, more able to bounce back from trouble."

There is a very successful way to develop an appreciation in your kids for what they look like. Often, kids criticize their looks too much and feel bad about how their body is shaped. This can be extremely demotivating for them and can become a big challenge if not treated properly. Experts give an easy solution for this issue by advising the parents to set a good example at home.

The Child Development Institute explained the following:

"Your children pay attention to what you say and do — even if it does not seem like it sometimes. If you are always complaining about your weight or feel pressure to change your body shape, your children may learn that these are important concerns. If you are attracted to new "miracle" diets, they may learn that restrictive dieting is better than making healthy lifestyle choices. If you tell your daughter that she would be prettier if she lost weight, she will learn that the goals of weight loss are to be attractive and accepted by others. The same stands for a son being told he would be more handsome if he had bigger muscles. Reinforcement of these superficial ideals suggests that physical attributes are the most important features of a person.

Parents are role models and should try to follow the healthy eating and physical activity patterns that you would like your children to follow — for your health and theirs. Extreme weight concerns and eating disorders, as well as obesity, are hard to treat. Yet, you can play an important role in preventing these problems for your children.

Having a healthy and positive body image means liking your body, appreciating it, and being grateful for its qualities and capabilities. When parents care for and appreciate their own bodies, they teach their kids to do the same.

Be a good role model. How you talk about your own looks sets a powerful example. Constantly complaining about or fretting over your appearance teaches your kids to cast the same critical eye on themselves. Almost everyone is dissatisfied with certain elements of their appearance but talk instead about what your body can do, not just how it looks. Instead of griping about how big your legs are, talk about how they are strong enough to help you hike up a mountain."

2. Bullying and Peer Pressure

Teens are influenced by their peers more than anyone because they spend a large part of their day with them and interact with them more than anyone. Peers have more influence on adolescents because they are from the same age group. So, your adolescent child is under the constant influence of his peers. He may not feel this, but it is happening. Though peer influence can bring good changes in your child like encouragement to perform better in studies and sports, at other times it can be negative, for example, getting involved in drugs and pot smoking.

Sherri Gordon wrote the following in *Verywell Family*, a modern resource online that offers a realistic and friendly approach to parenting and gives facts and guidance for parents to feel confident about the choices they make for themselves and their families:

> "Peer pressure is pressure from others to conform to the behaviors, attitudes and personal habits of a group or clique. Sometimes kids within a clique will pressure other kids to participate in bullying. This bullying can include everything from leaving mean notes and name-calling to sabotaging another person's relationship with gossip, lies, and rumors. In

fact, a lot of relational aggression and cyberbullying involves peer pressure.

Other times, tweens and teens will feel an internal pressure to do things they think their peers are doing. For instance, some kids will participate in sexting because they think everyone else is doing it too. In other words, peer pressure causes kids to do things they would not otherwise do with the hope of fitting in or getting attention.

Typically, when kids give in to peer pressure it is because they want to be liked or fit in. They fear that if they do not go along with the group or clique, then other kids might make fun of them. As a result, bullying sometimes is an act of self-preservation. Kids are afraid if they do not exclude others, participate in gossip, spread rumors and make fun of others, then they too will be ostracized or tormented by bullies.

Additionally, some kids accept the idea that "everyone's doing it" and often mistakenly feel less responsibility for bullying when it is done as a group. With this type of pack mentality, kids often leave their better judgment and common sense behind. As a result, they do not feel as much remorse as they would otherwise."

Parents have got the power to change their kids, although they often feel they cannot. In fact, they can change much in their lives because of their status of being parents. The teens show strength and independence, but they still need their parents. So, do not miss the chance to step in and play your role.

Even teachers have a big place in the minds of teens. With their style of teaching, assisting the students, and sharing good thoughts, teachers can induce several good views in the minds of teens. It is the sharing and caring style of teachers that makes the teens feel comfortable enough to talk to them and also listen to what they say.

Gordon further advised the following:

"Talk to your kids. Try to understand the pressures they are experiencing. Ask them about the pressures they feel to engage in relational aggression, cyberbullying and other forms of bullying. The more you can connect with your kids about bullying, the more you will be able to have a positive influence. Give your kids ideas on how to respond to peer pressure. And be sure they are equipped with solid self-esteem, assertiveness skills, and social skills. These traits help kids respond to peer pressure in a positive way.

If you have a policy of not bullying others and you find out your child is a bully — even if he was pressured into it — you have to follow through with disciplinary actions. If you do not, your child will assume that the rules do not apply or are not a big deal. As a result, the bullying may escalate to the point that it gets out of control or seriously harms another person. Remember, looking the other way only harms your child in the end."

Does all the talking and sharing mean that no bullying will happen?

No, you need to understand that bullying is inevitable, but leaving it unchecked is the real problem. It is not a problem if you find your teen in his early teen years or later bullying someone at school. Do not feel upset and let yourself lose control of your temper. Do not yell at your kid or criticize. Help him analyze what he did and take responsibility for his behavior.

If you find that your kid had become rude and harsh, encourage him to apologize as a civilized citizen. Even if the bullying act did not hurt a child at school, but damaged some property like covering a wall with graffiti, talk to your child to amend it. The point is to encourage your child to understand that any damaging behavior needs to be followed by a remedy from him.

Another very important point in here is to avoid labeling your child a bully. Talk to him about the opposite behavior, which is based on consideration, kindness, forgiveness, and tolerance. Do not keep remembering his bullying acts.

This is not one day and night's job. It will take time until good understanding seeps into the mind of your child. But, continue with your positive talks and good communication. You need to help him learn to take positive and good decisions while facing peer pressure.

There are some mistakes that you should avoid. When your child is involved in bullying along with his friends, do not start planning to choose his friends. Give your child enough imagination and understanding of friends, and leave him to choose his friends. It is quite possible that while he is friends with some kid, he does not fall under his influence, and knows how to act smart.

Moreover, you need to set some rules which are strictly followed at home by all the family members including parents. These rules can help you and your child stay away from a number of problems.

The Child Development Institute recommended the following:

> "Set clear rules and boundaries for your teen. Make sure they know ahead of time what they are and are not allowed to do. Set a strict curfew and make sure they understand what the consequences will be if they break the rules. If they break the rules, be firm. When you make rules and do not stick to them, your child is less likely to follow them.
>
> Ask your teen where they are going and what they are doing. Take it upon yourself to make sure they are where they say they are. This does not mean you need to follow them around town, but you should call parents of the friends they are going with and double check the plans and just to ensure they are safe. You may also consider getting them a cell phone so they can check in every so often. While you may think your children will feel oppressed by this behavior, they will also know you care what happens and feel more responsible about keeping out of unsafe situations."

Bullying and peer pressure are often linked together. Parents feel worried and helpless about what goes on at school and how to make it less worrying. Of course, there is no way that you can put an end to it, but you can "tame" the situation to a great extent.

Since your child is directly dealing with his classmates and friends, you need to expand his understanding of how to deal with peer pressure and stay away from being bullied and bullying.

Teach your child that it is okay to say no in situations that do not seem okay. Peer pressure can be strong, but not stronger than the willpower of a person. Often teens never say no to their friends and that is why they are not aware of the fact that it is okay to say no and still be friends with your peers.

Peers can put any sort of pressure on each other including bullying, doing drugs, drinking, smoking pot, and watching porn. These activities are against the ethics of every family and parents can easily train their kids to say no to such things. When parents set expectations for the overall behavior of family members and set values, their kids understand well that these are the limits that they should not cross.

Some parents complain that they had set all the family values and ethics, but their kids easily fall to the peer pressure. In such cases, parents should check for loopholes; maybe parents are so strict that kids do not confide in them. Maybe there are issues at home like fights between the parents, which shatter the confidence of kids in the family values.

For example, your daughter was late last night while she was coming back from her friend's birthday party. Where she was? How did she come home? At what time did she leave her friend's house?

Tell her that, next time, if it is going to be very late, she can avoid attending the party. You can also call the friend's parents and share your concerns. Next time, stay in communication with the parents of the kid who has invited your kid to a party or a hangout. This will encourage your kid to say no when things go against the family rules.

Often, kids fall under peer pressure because they find others more confident in their decisions. This lack of self-esteem and confidence can be the direct reason why your child is easy to pressurize.

Just feeling strongly about making a decision of their own does not mean they dare to make it. Sometimes they feel better to let their peers make the decision. Many times they know in their heart what they should do, but do not have enough courage to say it out loud.

3. Anxiety and Depression

Teen depression is increasing. Parents need to know the key skills to help their child handle his anxiety. Since this is a psychological disorder, it can be complicated to treat it. But, be it anxiety or an injury in the body, the first key tool is to have the belief that it is curable. Experts call it "positive expectancy."

The teen years can be extremely challenging and anxiety can cause damage to the adolescents more than we can understand. It has been calculated through studies that one out of every five adolescents from all social backgrounds suffers from anxiety and depression at some point during their adolescence. However, the unfortunate fact is that while anxiety and depression are highly treatable, most teens never get any treatment for these.

Lynn Lyons, a licensed clinical social worker and psychotherapist in Concord, New Hampshire, specializing in the treatment of anxiety disorders in adults and children, wrote the following on her website of the same name:

"As an anxiety expert, I often talk to teens who are also depressed. Why?

Because an untreated anxiety disorder in a child is one of the top predictors of developing depression as a teen or young adult, a fact that most teens and parents are unaware of. And because anxiety is the chief mental health complaint of young people, it's not surprising that rates of depression in teens are increasing.

Adolescence is often the time when longer-term issues with anxiety and worry become more intense and isolating. The challenges of social life and increased academic pressures push kids toward brand new experiences and responsibilities, along with the shadow side of hesitation and insecurity.

Specific learning difficulties can surface as students take on more complicated tasks or have to speak up in class. Sports become more demanding, and hormones can wreak havoc with appearance. Whether social, intellectual or physical, anything can serve as a source of worry.

Teens are caught between wanting to achieve and being afraid of failing, of wanting to belong and fearing rejection.

To make matters worse, teens are developmentally more likely to reject adult input as they strive to be independent and find their own answers. At the very time when they are faced with huge changes — graduating from high school, waiting to hear from colleges, moving away from home or deciding on a career path — your advice and desire to help are met with resistance.

No degree of reassurance or encouragement seems to be enough because you cannot give your teen what she's looking for: a guarantee that everything will turn out perfectly."

So, the desire of finding a certain answer to every worry brings the anxiety into action and your teen becomes forever anxious. Moreover, the intricacies of the social world grab the teens from another end and they remain hanging between hopelessness, withdrawal, and uncertainty.

So, what can be done?

Helping teens is immensely important. Only close adults like parents and teachers can catch up with the condition of teens and help them normalize the challenges of relationships and uncertainty.

So, how can we help?

Lyons suggested the following in the same article "Teen, Anxiety and Depression":

> "What can you as a parent do to help? You can start by paying attention to how you and your family handle failure and mistakes.
>
> Research tells us convincingly that your own relationship with anxiety and uncertainty — and how you role model this to your child — significantly impacts how she sees the world. When is something good enough? How do you move on to your next task? What does your family say about screw-ups?
>
> Now may be the time to notice and change your own response to mistakes, to sprinkle family conversation with phrases that normalize screw-ups, struggles, and imperfection.
>
> Teens also need to hear that they aren't expected to know everything and that they can't see into the future.
>
> Flexibility is key, and this means knowing when to push harder and when to be satisfied with a less-than-perfect result. As you see your teen becoming anxious, look for opportunities

to let her know that this IS a time of uncertainty, but you have confidence in her ability to problem solve along the way.

Giving advice about how you would handle things might not be as valuable as instilling a sense of autonomy in your teen — and this may mean backing off the lectures and letting her know that you are there to support her as she makes HER choices.

Help teens to step back from their rigid expectations and permanent mindset, and instead support them through this time of struggle, discomfort, discovery, and growth with the language of change, possibility, and movement.

Most importantly, stay connected to your teens, even when they are being clear about how annoying you are.

Small gestures go a long way: offer a compliment, ask question or two that conveys genuine interest, and be that steady stream of messages that let them know you are there when needed as they trip, fall, regroup, and find their path.

Finally, teens need to hear that they are supposed to be anxious! Expecting to be calm and relaxed during such a time of change is unrealistic. In fact, moving toward anxiety and learning how to manage it is the skill I most strongly promote."

4. Health and Drugs

This is the scariest challenge that your teens face. You fear it the most, yet many parents do not know how to deal with this issue. Although common awareness is sufficiently widespread that drugs kill and smoking impairs health, the adolescents still find shelter in drugs, weed, tobacco, etc.

According to a survey by the Centers for Disease Control and Prevention (CDC), drugs are the most difficult issue for adolescents. In Singapore, *The Straits Times* reported in 2017 that 151 young Singaporeans and permanent residents studying in primary to tertiary public educational institutions were caught for drug offenses, up from 124 in 2015 and 83 in 2014.

The National Academies of Sciences, Engineering, and Medicine published a workshop report titled "Challenges in Adolescent Health Care" (2007), which reported the following:

"The most difficult issues many adolescents confront in their daily lives — from questions about sexuality and experimentation with drugs and alcohol to emotional problems, obesity, or anorexia — are or could easily turn into health problems that can persist throughout their adult lives. And the adolescents who are frequently most disconnected from routine health care services — those who lack insurance or who lack parental guidance and family support — are frequently the ones who are at greatest risk for multiple and chronic health problems.

A significant proportion of adolescents' health problems relate to sexual activity; use of tobacco, alcohol, and illicit drugs; driving while impaired; poor diet; mental disorders; and exposure to weapons, according to the CDC's Youth Risk Behavior Survey and the Substance Abuse and Mental Health Services Administration's National Survey on Drug Use and Health."

Parents need to start talking about this issue with their kids at home from the start of their adolescence. Discussing drugs and other similar products is the only way to start implanting awareness in the brain of your kids.

Before the kids reach that developed stage when they have the courage to consider drugs and accept them either on their own or under peer pressure, they have enough knowledge with them that can work as a safeguard against wrong decisions.

So, you get started with the facts and get them from authentic well-trusted resources. Remember to give your kids ONLY factual information and true knowledge. If you are not sure of a fact, hold on to it until you are sure. Adults, especially parents, enjoy a respected status in the hearts and minds of their kids. Giving incomplete, wrong, or fictitious information can hurt your status. Moreover, your kid loses trust in you and no longer believes in you.

There are other things which are equally important for you and your kids. These are not facts about drugs, but these are your cultural values and family rules, your community ethics, your own experience, and knowledge. These hold equal sanctity to you and your child. You can include them in your talking sessions and your communication with your kids about substance abuse.

Your best point to start with is health and its importance in life. Good health is an easy topic which you can get started on with younger kids as well. This can be a strong base to build on with regard to the awareness of substance abuse as well.

You strike the discussion on health quite often and keep it an ongoing topic in your family life. Show practically that you are interested in taking care of your health and avoid things that are toxic to your health.

Frequent discussions at suitable times (do not talk on a party night) are helpful in clarifying values and rules to your kids. Long conversations that are spread out over several months or maybe years are always helpful in bringing good results. If you talk for a while and expect your kids to comply, they would not because they will feel like it is your effort to control them.

But, do not worry if you are one of those parents who have got the message late, you can still get started even if it is late. You can make the whole discussion focused on Why drugs? Why substance abuse? Why avoid? Why take caution?

Show your honesty and love your teens. They understand the emotions of honesty and love. So, your efforts to keep them safe and doing well in life with perfect health will be clear to them.

It is not that you don't trust them. It is not that you want to ruin their fun. You love them. And, you want to keep them physically and emotionally safe.

The Center for Parent and Teen Communication states the following:

> "Listen to what your tweens and teens have to say about substances. They likely know more than you think they do. Listening is the key to getting teens to talk to us. Fewer words coming from us often means more coming from them.
>
> Young people ask questions to get trusted information or clarification. Do not assume if they ask a question about certain substances that they must be using them or are somehow involved with them. Questions are good. Sometimes they are just curious or have heard others talking about it. It is

important they get accurate information. Be factual in the responses you offer. If asked a question you are unable to answer, say you will work to get answers and get back to them.

We should not assume our teens understand everything we tell them. Ask them to repeat back what they've heard us say. "I've just thrown a lot of information at you. What did you take away from what I said?" If it seems like they've misunderstood, try reframing the information."

To help you, find related TV shows, movies, inspiring documentaries, book websites, and awareness programs in your community to let your teens get ample support and motivation, which fortify them against substance abuse.

More awareness and solid beliefs come from frequent and repeated encounters with factual information, real live incidents, interviews of experts and people who had personal experiences, etc.

Once you are able to start the flow of discussions and information provision in a smooth and regular manner, you will feel relief that your teens have better awareness.

5. Sex and Romance

Teens hit puberty at the start of their adolescence. Their body changes. Sexual maturation starts its process. This process is highly influential on a person and it is marked by increases of chemicals that regulate the body functions all over. These hormones are of various sorts and they help the body grow stronger, taller, more muscular, and the sexual regions of the body become active.

Following the start of puberty, sex hormones become active and circulate all over the body. Sexual desires awaken and strengthen in teens. The feelings of attraction toward the opposite gender become active and erotic arousal becomes frequent.

Sex is an intense challenge; it has negative effects when practiced at an early age or outside the context of marriage.

The changes that happen from the onset of puberty and sexuality create an immense challenge for adolescents. They long for intimacy and the desire to feel further what sex is becomes more and more intense.

Being parents, our best strategy for our teens at this stage of life is to stay present. Communicate with your teens and make them comfortable at home and trigger talks that are educational, informational, and elaborate with facts.

There are several resources for educating kids on sex. But, these are considered external resources and cannot be equal to parental education on sex in their efficiency. Sutter Health Palo Alto Medical Foundation recommended the following:

"Talking about sexuality with your children can be a challenge. Sometimes parents are fearful about saying too much, too soon (although there's no evidence that this should be a concern). Some parents feel they don't know enough to be a reliable source of accurate information. Additionally, when teens feel uncomfortable coming to their parents or guardians regarding difficult issues, such as sex, they often turn to their friends and/or the media in order to gain information.

Quick Facts

- Parents are the most important sexuality educators for their children.
- No parent needs to be an expert on sexuality to have meaningful conversations with their children — parents can share their values about sexuality, relationships, and respect for others.
- Some parents believe that talking about sex will lead to teens having sex. In fact, research shows that teens who have talked with their parents about sex are more likely to postpone sex.
- Teens that have high self-esteem are more likely to make responsible decisions about sex.
- Teens often believe that all of their friends are having sex. This belief puts pressure on teens (especially boys) to have sex.
- Every 1 in 350 teens contract a sexually transmitted disease (STD).
- The United States of America has one of the highest (teens) birth rates among developing countries.
- Teens often overestimate the percentage of their peers that are sexually experienced.

Topics to Talk About

The following is a list of important topics relating to sex and sexuality. Although your teen may have some concept of these topics due to the media, school, friends, etc. it is important to discuss these topics with your teen 1-on-1. Chances are, your teen could be severely misinformed regarding these issues — you cannot assume that your teen is already well educated regarding any of these issues.

- Male & Female Reproductive Systems
- Sexual Intercourse
- Pregnancy
- Abstinence/Postponing Sex

- Ways to Show Affection Without Having Sex
- Birth Control
- Family Planning
- Correct Sexual Orientation (Heterosexual, homosexual, bisexual, transsexual, etc.)
- HIV/AIDS and other STDs
- Recognition of sexual abuse
- Emotional Consequences of Sex – rape (such as date rape, gay rape, etc.), sexual assault, sexual abuse, etc.
- Emotional Consequences of Sexual
- Violence
- [Relating to the last two topic] Happiness in married life (how to avoid or recognize sexual abuse, sexual violence, etc.)
- How Alcohol and Other Drugs Affect Decisions

How to Talk with Your Teen about Sex
Be clear about your values
Before you speak with your child about sexuality, think about what your values are. What do you believe? What does your faith tradition say? It is important to give your children factual information — and to be very specific about how your beliefs either agree with or differ from what is scientifically possible.

Talk about facts vs. beliefs
Sometimes, factual information can challenge a personal belief or what a faith community believes. This can provide an opportunity to make sure that your child both has accurate information and hears what your values are relating to it. It also provides an opportunity to explain that there are different beliefs in the community, that people are allowed to disagree with each other, and that differing views should be respected — as long as those views are based on ethics, responsibility, justice, equality, and nonviolence.

Practice what you preach
Young people often find it confusing when parents talk about a value regarding sexuality and then act in a way that does not support that value. Some common values about sexuality and relationships that most people support include honesty, equality, responsibility, and respect for differences. Acting on your values and being a good role model are powerful messages for your children. On the other hand, your beliefs will not seem very important or valuable to your children if they don't see you respect and abide by them yourself.

But don't preach
Have a conversation with your children — do not talk at them. Find out what they think and how they feel about sexuality and relationships. Then you will be able to share information and respond to questions in ways that will resonate with the belief system they are developing for themselves.

Encourage a sense of pride
All children deserve to be wanted and loved, and parents can reinforce this message. Let them know you are interested in what they think and how they feel about any topic, whether it is sexuality, school, religion, the future, or whatever. When your children share feelings with you, praise them for it. Correct misinformation gently, and reinforce your values whenever possible.

Keep the conversation going
Too often, parents think they need to wait until they collect enough information and energy to be prepared to have "THE TALK" with their children. However, sexuality is a part of every person's life from the moment he or she is born. It is important, therefore, to start the conversation early, and to make it clear to your children that you are always willing to

talk about sexuality — whenever questions come up for them, or when a "teachable moment" occurs.

Keep your sense of humor!
Sexuality, in most of its aspects, can be a joyful topic for discussion in the family. Remember to keep your sense of humor throughout conversations with your child — the conversation does not have to be tense and uncomfortable unless you make it that way.

SHOULD WE LET OUR TEENS PRACTICE SEX?

There remains a big question that many parents ask about their adolescents when it comes to talking about sex.

Experts have different opinions regarding the answer to this question. Some opine that teens must be directed to fight the urge or peer pressure to practice sex. Pediatrician Dr. Ron Eagar was quoted (healthychildren.org) in the article "Helping Teens Resist Sexual Pressure" as stating the following:

> "The pressure on teenagers to have sex is enormous, kids often feel as if they are caught in a vice. Not only do they have to contend with the direct pressure to "do it" from their date or steady boyfriend/girlfriend, there is the peer pressure applied by friends who want to know (elbow jab, wink wink) "didja do it?" They may also feel the internal pressure to keep pace with their friends as if competing in a marathon to lose their virginity. One way of helping them resist these pressures is to anticipate them and discuss them."

Dan Seigel has a more modern vision of sex or as it is now called, "Hook up."

He calls sex the "realization of sex life without the wish of pair bonding." He further explained the following:

> "Our biological legacy is to move from sexual immaturity during the pre-adolescent years to sexual maturity in the adolescent and adult years. How we experience and express those sexual feelings will be shaped by our temperament, our family, our friends, and our culture. Let's remember, too, that in our evolutionary past, there was a much quicker transition that bridged the divide between sexual immaturity and adult responsibility.
>
> By the time physiological sexual maturity happened in the middle to late teens, we were socially set up to make sexual connections with others and ready to make babies. Now we have a prolonged period of adolescence in which sexual feelings emerge with maturation but pair bonding (finding a mate and creating a new family home) does not occur until much, much later. In modern cultures today, these informal sexual connections sometimes shape how an adolescent first realizes his or her sexual life."

However, youth who had experienced this and passed the phase of adolescence, have a mixed reaction to this question. *Health Children* (healthchildren.org) states the following:

> "Researchers in New Zealand interviewed nearly one thousand young people, all in their mid-twenties, about their first sexual experiences. On average, the men had become sexually active when they were seventeen; the women, at age sixteen. Looking back, more than half the women admitted that they now wished they'd held onto their virginity longer, a

sentiment seconded by 70 percent of the women who had been fifteen or younger the first time they had intercourse."

The question remains open for all parents to answer as they find appropriate for their teens. There are family values, cultural boundaries, social manners, health issues, kids' mental and psychological conditions, and religious limits that determine for every youth which path he has to take.

But, the role of parents remains crucial in the life of their kids by clearing doubts about sex and explaining things sufficiently. There are several things that teachers can also contribute to in terms of knowledge and understanding. The opportunity to elaborate on details which are important for the kids arises several times during their school years. Teachers should not shy away from the topic and close it, especially when it is related to the lessons.

That is why it is important that adults do a widespread study of the topic so as to explain it to the kids in a way that makes them understand it as a practice that must be safe.

Parents who want to train their daughters on refraining from sex must train them on how to say no and stay strong in their choice.

With some practice of replies and dialogues, you can make them understand how to resist a guy who is urging them to comply with their desire.

Here is a set of responses that a girl can use as a guiding table when it comes to rejecting the offer:

Hook	Sinker
"Aw c'mon, everybody does it!"	"I don't care, I'm not everybody. And besides, not everybody 'does it,' including some of the kids who say they do."
"If you loved me, you'd go to bed with me."	"If you loved me, you wouldn't pressure me into doing something that I'm not ready to do."
"If you don't have sex with me, I'll break up with you."	"If being your girlfriend means that I have to sleep with you, then I guess I don't want to be your girlfriend."
"Why won't you have sex with me?"	"Because I don't want to." No further explanation needed.
"We had sex before; why are you turning me down now?"	"I'm entitled to change my mind. It's my body and my life, and I want to wait until I'm older before I have sex again."
"Yo, let's do it. You know you want to!"	"No. No. No! What part of 'no' don't you understand?"
"Your parents are out all night; let's go back to your house."	Use your ace in the hole: blame your folks. "Go back to my house? We can't. My parents won't let me have boys over when they're not home."

Last Updated 11/2/2009
Source Caring for Your Teenager (Copyright © 2003 American Academy of Pediatrics)

The bigger part of this challenge is when your adolescent kid shares with you her immense love for a guy. As a caring and loving parent, you feel obliged to do ensure several things. This is natural and should be present in the mind and heart of every parent.

Dan Seigel mentions a girl Sara who would come to him for therapy. Sara fell in love with a guy called Jared and shared the whole matter with her father. Her father wanted to meet Jared. She told her therapist the following:

"He just needed to see who Jared is so he could know I wasn't being hurt by this guy."

As a father, I know that feeling of wanting to be protective while also wanting to support. **It's the parental challenge of being a safe harbor and a launching pad all at once.** It's not so easy sometimes."

Yes, parental care is of great importance and teens' safety depends on their parents.

Here, you can imagine how much you should be aware of your obligations and responsibilities toward your kids to help them grow into happy and satisfied adults.

SUMMARY

1. How each adolescent approaches challenges differs based on their growing environment and cultural boundaries.
2. The challenges that youth encounter are biological, cognitive, and psychological in nature.
3. Five key challenges that youth undergo are as follows:
   a. Drastic physical changes in their body followed by a constant struggle to accept these changes.
      i. Parents help their youth by teaching them to appreciate their own body, developing healthy lifestyles, and being good role models themselves.
   b. Struggles with negative peer pressure and bullying.
      i. Have open discussions with the youth and process their motivations behind negative behaviors.
      ii. Setting clear boundaries and following through on consequences in a firm, yet supportive manner.
      iii. Teach the youth about right decision-making and empower them to follow through amid negative peer pressure.

c. Struggles with anxiety and depression.
     i. Parents help their youth through conversations and managing setbacks in a manner that normalizes mistakes and imperfections.
     ii. Address any unrealistic expectations that the youth may have of themselves.
  d. Exposure to the dangers of substance abuse and possible health impairments.
     i. Parents should have open, factual discussions that address the dangers of substance abuse and the importance of physical health.
  e. Youth are charged with sexual desires and a propensity toward sexual acts.
     i. Parents should have open, factual discussions about sex and sexuality, ranging from the biological process and consequences to alternatives.
     ii. Talking about sex can be difficult. The following are some guidelines to facilitate the discussion:
        a. Being clear about your values
        b. Talking about facts vs. beliefs
        c. Practicing what you preach
        d. Refraining from preaching or lecturing
        e. Encouraging a sense of pride
        f. Keeping the conversation going
        g. Incorporating humor in discussions
4. The appropriateness of sex lies within the values, culture, and personal beliefs of the family. It is crucial for the adults to clear any doubts and help their youth make an informed decision in this matter.
5. If sex is undesired, parents need to train their youth on how to reject sexual advances firmly and resist peer pressure through the use of practice dialogues.

Chapter 15
Conclusion

We have come to the end of this book. We started by establishing the grounds that one really needs to understand and know if the strategy one is going to use with youth is a limbic strategy or a prefrontal strategy, and is one aware of when to use which strategy given the presenting reactions or behaviors from teenagers. Hopefully, having gone through the substantial amount of materials and some guidance, you are able to know when to use what strategy. Again, a rule of thumb holds that if your teenager is negatively limbic or emotional, you do not want to use prefrontal strategies or any negative emotions.

At the same time, we discussed that the period of adolescent starts from the age of 12 or earlier and runs to the age of 25 or later. But, this is just a rough marker; adolescence can be extended to an older age. The experts leave this point of the argument because there is no precise definition of age of adolescence.

Adolescence is truly a perplexing time and undeniably an amazing period too, especially when adolescents learn, change, make decisions, shoulder responsibilities, plan, etc. At this stage of life, the growing youth develop a set of behaviors, thoughts, beliefs, and personality traits that shape up their life until its end.

I would love to emphasize the fact in closing that as far as we are serious to learn and understand adolescent years, we need to act on the basis of scientific facts **only**. Myths and baseless suppositions that are surrounding youth life do not help.

In order to take off with a positive and objective start, and leave behind any misconceptions, let me debunk some myths about the youth that hinder our factual understanding. Unfortunately, these myths are quite widespread and cloud our minds each time we come to take a factual approach to the subject.

So, let me clear out from our mind the effects of prevailing myths to make a fresh start moving forward:

MYTH #1 — ADOLESCENTS GO CRAZY DUE TO RAGING HORMONES

Fact: Scientifically, there is nothing in the human body that can be titled as "raging hormones" — there are only developing or rising hormones. Some significant epigenetic changes happen during the growing period of adolescence in the reward section of the brain. Hence, the experience and feeling of the sexual drive are immensely intense. However, this is never cultivated as "raging hormones." This phrase is misguided and destructive.

MYTH # 2 — ADOLESCENCE IS A NEGATIVE TIME OF LIFE

Fact: Adolescence is the most constructive phase of our lives — neurologically and even biologically. Calling it negative or crazy means marginalizing the importance of this period of life. The factual approach to this subject is to enhance the upsides and decrease the downsides of the changes happening in the brain of the youth at this stage.

MYTH # 3 — ADOLESCENCE IS A TIME OF IMMATURITY

Fact: This is scientifically incorrect about the human brain. In fact, the human brain is going through the process of remodeling and not being immature. The youth learn fast at this stage, improve their focus, and start choosing intentionally (and most of the times through logic too). Hence, this is all about the impactful experience of remodeling.

MYTH # 4 — ADOLESCENCE IS A SYNONYM FOR THE TEENAGE YEARS

Fact: Adolescence is mostly about brain development which continues after the ending of teenage years to the mid-twenties and sometimes to the late twenties.

MYTH #5 — ADOLESCENCE IS COMPLICATED AND TOUGH, YOUTH WANT TO GET OVER IT QUICKLY

Fact: Adolescence is a highly productive phase. As an adult, the youth should be challenged to keep it going with all its creativity as long as possible to reap its benefits.

These were the myths, and the facts against them are clear. What about misconceptions? There are several misconceptions that make no sense, but since we have become used to hearing them, we take them as they are without bothering our brains with logic to weigh these.

One such misconception that Sheryl G. Feinstein, educator and author of *Secrets of the Teenage Brain*, talks about is that *the kids act weird because of hormones*:

> "Hormones are off the list of primary suspects! The teenagers-act-crazy because-of-hormones theory is incomplete. Think of it this way: Adults have hormones in their bodies, too, yet manage to write memos and grade homework even while thinking about a hot date later that evening. Adolescents are not victims of chemicals coursing through their veins and turning their fancies to thoughts of love or mayhem; if they have trouble sitting still in school and concentrating on their lesson plans, it's because their brains are not finished yet!"

So, instead of putting the blame on the hormones, we should study the brain development of the kids and find out the real causes of their specific mental state.

The human brain goes through developmental changes; it evolves, expands, strengthens, develops more abilities, etc. It is the changes in this stage of life that the adults have not yet been able to understand fully. The secrets of kids growing into adults are not fully revealed. The frustration of ignorance is leading the adults to misinterpret and make mistakes in analyzing.

Adults have become used to conceptualizing adolescents as wrongdoers, arrogant, crazy, irrational, etc. In fact, the reality is different. It is only the complicated changes that are not like an open book to us. But, scientific research and facts that have been discovered by the experts till date are an excellent resource for us to step out of our misconception.

The good and growth of every community depends on how adolescents are contributing to it. Adolescents have all the energy and even abilities to build families and even countries when they are appropriately engaged by adults. Hence, we need to understand adolescents!

SO, IN SUMMARY, WHAT IS ADOLESCENCE?

The adolescence is a fertile period of time which is filled with untouched potential. Hence, youth hold immense power in positive directions. Once parents start empowering the youth in this way, we can motivate them to accomplish far more than ever. In fact, we will just help their neural development bloom. So, let us embrace the adolescence as a period of creativity and incredible courage and never a phase of chaos and conflict.

FEATURES OF THE ADOLESCENT PERIOD

Daniel J. Siegel, author of *Brainstorm: The Power and Purpose of the Teenage Brain* and psychiatrist, describes the adolescent period with four vital features. He has arranged them in an acronym. He sees the *ESSENCE* of this period of life which is either ignored by society or buried under distraction and stress:

> **ES:** An *Emotional Spark* is revealed in the enhanced way emotion generated from sub-cortical areas washes over the cortical circuits of reasoning. The downsides are emotional storms and moodiness; the upside is a powerful passion to live life fully, to capture life being on fire.

SE: *Social Engagement* emerges as teens turn more toward peers than parents, the downside being falling prey to peer pressure center to gain membership in a group, the upside is the central importance of supportive relationships in our lives. Relationships are the key factor associated with medical and mental health, longevity, and even happiness.

N: *Novelty*-seeking emerges from shifts in the brain's dopamine system with the downside of risk-taking behavior and injury, and the upside of having the courage to leave the familiar, certain, and safe home nest for the unfamiliar, uncertain, potentially unsafe world beyond.

(At this stage the job of parents is to explain and guide their adolescents to listen to the signals inside them. They need to sense the changes in their gut-feeling. It is not important that they speak why something feels wrong. The most important is to understand the signals that are blinking danger from inside and respond appropriately).

CE: The *Creative Exploration* of adolescence is found as we push against the status quo, imagining how things could be, not simply accepting them for what they are. The downside? Not just conforming to life, as usual, can be disorienting and stressful. The upside? The thrill and passion of discovery — and the reality that most innovations in art, music, science, and technology emerge from the adolescent mind.

Our cultural attitude toward adolescents can foster, or inhibit, their movement toward becoming more and more integrated as individuals who are also integrated as members of a larger society, welcoming them to participate in how we shape our world. If we as adults can reclaim the ESSENCE of adolescence in our own lives, perhaps we'll find a natural way to recognize these factors and harness their upsides not only in ourselves but in adolescents as well.

Raising your kids into adolescents and adolescents into adults is a long journey. In fact, you start the right upbringing of your kids from day one when they first come into the world. At this early stage, the first thing to get started with is your love and only love.

Though the brain of your child is still quite small, she senses your love while you knit strong bonds of care, affection, closeness, warmth, and belonging.

With time, the brain of a child grows into a mature part of her body and she starts learning things in life while developing emotions and a sense of things.

The brain takes longer to become mature in the matter of logic and rationality.

Knowing the fact that an adolescent enjoys a more mature level of emotions earlier than logic can help parents and teachers tweak their style of training and alter their expectations, which often go beyond the power of adolescents.

This book is an effort to offer some detailed information on adolescent brain development and the challenges that adolescents face. Maybe this book can help countless adolescents to go through a happier adolescence period with their family and friends.

SUMMARY

1. Parents must base their understanding of youth behavior on scientific facts, rather than myths. Some prevailing myths are as follows:
    a. Adolescents go crazy due to raging hormones.
    b. Adolescence is a negative time of life.
    c. Adolescence is a time of immaturity.
    d. Adolescence is a synonym for the teenage years.
    e. Adolescence is complicated and tough, and youth want to get over it quickly.
2. Adolescence is a phase of untouched potential for the youth. It consists of four vital features that can be remembered in the acronym ESSENCE:
    a. ES — Emotional Spark
    b. SE — Social Engagement
    c. N — Novelty-seeking
    d. CE — Creative Exploration
3. Helping youth fulfill their potential in a positive manner is a process driven primarily by parental love, patience, and a mindful awareness of the youth's tendencies and developmental progress.

Real-Life Stories

CLIENT — JG

Back in school, I was neither the smartest student in the class, nor was I an obedient kid. Going to school for me was just another normal day of not knowing what the purpose was back then.

Following a typical daily routine to school meant going to classes to listen to what the teacher taught, sitting behind my desk pondering what my future will hold as I was in the lowest stream of my level, Normal Technical (NT).

It seemed that the world had nothing left for me to hold on to, nothing to look forward to, no dream or goal but deep down I knew that I really wanted to prove something to people but just didn't know where to begin.

Growing up in a broken family was even more depressing as the basic guidance or foundation was never taught to me at home. My parents were divorced when I was young. Court Custody was given to my father, but he was never there much for me, and he would excuse himself due to his workload, leaving me to my grandmother who raised me, making sure that I was well-fed to get through the day.

At times, I would wonder why other families were so different compared to mine, having their parents help them with school tuition, homework, projects, or fetching them from school and activities such as swimming classes, or even going for a vacation during year-end school holidays.

I wondered what I did wrong that caused people around me not to care for and love me. Not being able to share my feeling whenever I am happy or sad. This makes me feel as if I had done something wrong, which resulted in not having people around to love and care for me. I was unable to share my feelings with anyone.

I came to a point of having suicidal thoughts, why not end all this by jumping off the building so I won't be feeling depressed and helpless anymore. However, I was lucky enough not to execute it after all.

Eventually, I sought attention somewhere else. This was when I started mixing with the wrong group of friends, seeking a sense of belonging at that point. Having them praise you and cheer for you even when you are doing the wrong stuff, guiding you to try new stuff even when you know it is illegal.

Picking up cigarettes was the first baby step when you mix with the wrong group. Wanting the group to accept you as part of them, to feel cool, or to act like a grown up. This was followed by playing truant in school, mixing with other students from other schools who had the same character as you.

That was where the crucial part came in — joining a street gang; being part of the gang is like a second family. They would listen to you and understand how you feel, because most of the members had the same family issues. Since our parents cannot bring enjoyment to us, during the school holidays, we would create our own enjoyment in our own ways.

We would hang out by the arcades and get ourselves into fights with other groups, and with little or no money left, what were we to do? We would go around stealing people's belongings such as wallets and phones that were unattended. On some occasions, we would challenge one another to steal items from shops in the shopping mall in order to feel the excitement of running away from the security guards while having your group members cheer for you while they are waiting at the end point.

Falling into the spiral, it no longer mattered to me how people would judge me as long I got more attention from my friends to fit in or got acceptance from them. After a period of time of being the opposite of how you should behave, you start having people judge you and being labeled as the bad student in school.

One day, a new lesson was introduced to us in class while I was attending school. We were wondering what additional subject we would have to learn. A group of adults came into the class and left everyone pondering what kind of subject required three teachers.

That is where my life actually started to turn around. One of the representatives left a deep impression on me, which I will never forget. This is what he said: "I know many of you felt that ending up in this stream, Normal Technical (NT), due to poor academic results is making you feel worthless and want to be rebellious and no longer wish to focus on your studies. But, let me tell you this, every individual is unique and special in different ways and able to create their own craft, but that only depends on what kind of decision you wish to make, it is either for the better or for the worse. Your choice!"

For the first time after hearing these "speeches," his words really pierced my heart, leaving me hanging for a while; having someone believe in us, not judging us based on what classes we are from, is truly refreshing.

They were a group of professional youth workers, helping youth like me reach their highest potential. Basically, they were helping students who might have low self-esteem issues and working hand in hand with us, giving us another opportunity to redefine ourselves. Looking at a different aspect of our lives to cultivate us through encouragement. Just imagine a basketball team — we are the players and they are the coaches, finding our weaknesses and strengths, and training us to be the best version of ourselves.

The lessons they had for us were not just the typical lessons you get from teachers. The lessons were designed in a much more interactive ways, free style, and most importantly they would ask our opinions on things and they wanted to hear from us.

They had journal booklets that require you to write your goals, helping you keep track of how much progress you have been making throughout the week. Also, they had methods to enable you to make better decisions, such as Specific, Measurable, Achievable, Realistic, Time (S.M.A.R.T) goals.

They had after-school interest group activities for us to join in, such as music and drama. Using music to express our feelings is one of the ways to calm us down, and after that we were invited to share our thoughts or even a week in our personal life, thereby coming together as a group to help out one another.

One of the aims I guess was to distract us from mixing with the wrong groups and having someone to fall back on who you can really rely on. I could see that everyone in my class was enjoying the lesson and the company of the youth workers. They always reminded us that we could always look for them if we needed help. Years went by, and holding on to what I have learnt from their classes, I entered into the workforce.

On a random occasion, I crossed paths once again with this special youth worker who once taught me in Secondary Two. He was affectionately known to us as Mr. Nick. We did some catching up and he shared many stories with me about his work with youth.

He refreshed my memory again about what I had gone through during my days in secondary school with the team he was with. Having him once again in my life, he guided me with his knowledge and allowed me to apply myself in my work and personal life

This has transformed me into a better leader and better father than I could ever be. Using methods to better understand my co-workers, motivating them to do the work that is needed to be done. A better listening ear to my child, understanding his emotional needs, giving him a much more meaningful childhood, which I did not have in my younger days.

Mr. Nick was not just a youth worker to me but a role model to look up to. A mentor who will continue to give me guidance throughout my life, to be the best version I can be each day.

To me, a youth worker is essentially important in today's context, as the stress levels are getting higher due to stronger competition in our society. Parents may not be able to foresee the attention which is required for our children.

In some schools, our teens may have youth workers work alongside them in their classes, and they may help our teens understand themselves better with specially designed lessons and or workshops. Youth workers have a much better understanding of mental well-being, and I wish there could be more around to reach out to youth who feel alone, lost, confused, and even without a purpose in their lives.

CLIENT — LH

I am currently working in the Education sector managing events. Prior to being in the education sector, I have always been working in events; this includes a multitude of event types from sporting to corporate events. Some of these would include the Standard Chartered Marathon Singapore, Regional Meetings from various organizations, and even fully virtual events. Apart from events, I also graduated with a bachelor's degree in science, Psychology.

During my time in the national service, I had the privilege of serving as an officer of the Republic of Singapore Air Force. I was given the opportunity to learn and apply what I have experienced about leadership in my scope of work. I was also appointed to be part of the Executive Committee in Republic Polytechnic's Student Council during my course of study.

There were definitely many experiences and people that touched my life and helped shape it the way it is today. Many of these experiences were not only from school curriculum but also external youth workers. Having youth workers take time off to impact youths, it certainly did me a lot of good when I got to interact with them during my lower secondary school days. One of the key highlights was being part of the High Impact Change Agent Leaders (HI-CAL) program.

I recall vividly years ago when I was in secondary school during an assembly where a group of instructors walked into the hall sharing a program known as HI-CAL. This was all very foreign to us, to hear that we could provoke change and we needed to make a change every once in a while was intriguing. This program was not only a 3-day and 2-night camp but there was also an ongoing project after the camp to see how we make change, how we lead each other on toward a common goal.

HI-CAL also focused largely on leadership — what it means to be a leader, how to be a leader, and most importantly, what it feels like to be a leader. Having so many different characters and personalities within each group, it definitely taught me how to assess situations when I needed to step up to take the lead and when I should take a backseat.

Through "Camp HI-CAL," four amazing volunteer mentors, Jun, Leonard, Yifen, and Dawei, together with a staff Nick guided me through so many types of scenarios and helped me understand leadership, service-learning, and even how we would go about getting grants and writing proposals for our project.

Before the HI-CAL program started, I was a very quiet and reserved individual; it always took me a while to start interacting with others, let alone take the lead in the group. The opportunities that my mentors gave me throughout the project made me realize how easy it was to step up as long as I wanted to do it and did not give up.

The program definitely lit a spark in me, helping me pursue my interest in leadership roles. The mentors and Nick were always there throughout the project and that itself was a very powerful gesture; I was happy to have them to lean on when I was in trouble. Through the few months of planning and executing a fundraising plan, we had many ups and downs, some of which made me feel like giving up as I was very frustrated about problems beyond my control.

This was when Nick, Leonard, and Dawei taught me that these were inevitable, but as long as we pick ourselves up and keep pushing, we will get there. When the project ended, I felt that the impact we made with the fundraiser was insignificant as it did not amount to much in terms of our contributions. Looking back now, I think that it achieved much more than just that; it made me want to explore more leadership roles and see how far I could go.

Beyond the project, Nick was more than a mentor to me; he became a friend who would check up on me occasionally to see how I was doing. Through many stages of my life, he has encouraged me to be positive, to take things in stride, and to learn from what I might see as "just another failure." I am very grateful for the contributions HI-CAL made in my life. From a simple project, it has since changed to become a pillar and support system for me through my youth.

CLIENT — DD

I have been a youth worker for over ten years. During this time, I have journeyed and walked with youth during their growing years. It was a decision that I would make again in a heartbeat.

The work has not only allowed me to improve the lives of youths but also improve my relationship with my mother. I chose this profession because I saw the joy in the lives of youth, and I wanted to be part of that. I could connect with it.

When we speak about our purpose, we would think about where we can fit in. Where would I be accepted, recognized, and heard?

These are the questions I would ask myself when asking who I am and what I was born to do. The answer lies in the stories and experiences of our lives.

Being brought up single-handedly by my mum, we faced a lot of obstacles together. Thus, social welfare and being supported by the system were very much a part of my life. In my experience, there were two aspects of need. One, which was obvious, was the need for resources to further my capacity to be part of society, such as money and skill set.

The other need is the social–emotional need to interact with society.

What is truly important in this work while helping people with gaps in their lives materialistically is relationships. Without it, the meaning of the work we do is lost.

That was my journey as a hot-headed, emotional, and impulsive kid. There was this dying thirst to be recognized, accepted, and to be valued as a person. This came from trauma from my past of abuse and abandonment. Because I struggled with my value, I translated this void through aggression and anger. I was not good in school as I was constantly getting into trouble.

I was seen as the bad kid with an attitude problem. One of my teachers even said I was a bad influence on others and would often tell parents to tell their kids to be wary of me. This caused a deeper resentment toward people. How would a 12-year-old kid, who had struggled with broken relationships, being told that he was toxic to others feel? I wanted the world to hear my cry, but I felt they ostracized me for my wounds.

Some key people played a role in my life, because they dared to step into my messed up world. In secondary school, my temper blew in class, and one of the teachers, Ms. Sharon Ng, witnessed this. She called me out and rather than scolding me, she sat with me calmly and attended to my anger. I felt heard and listened to. She referred me for anger management counseling where my journey toward healing began. It was here that I met with Mr. Nick, Dr. John, and Ms. Sue.

One of the lessons I learned was the lesson of self-talk. We hear and see many words day-in and day-out, and subconsciously those words impact us negatively and positively. I was told to pretend to be a tree in an activity. I closed my eyes and imagined myself as a tree while Mr. Nick spoke negative words.

These words were what I would hear growing up that shaped the angry broken me. Words like I was alone, unwanted, abandoned, stupid, etc. They were the realities I faced, though not the truth of who I was. I became the manifestation of those words and experiences that I faced over those years. Could you blame a boy who could not take care of himself to be shaped by the brokenness of the world?

I felt weak and I saw myself shaking in the storm. I was struggling to hold on to the ground. From a third-person perspective, I would be scared to go near this tree during the storm, because it would look scary and violent in the storm. Later, Mr. Nick spoke words of affirmation to me. Words of empowerment, such as "I'm capable and I'm strong," and I saw my roots firmly reaching down to the truths of who I am. This simple exercise helped me to ground myself to firmly believe that I am good. It built humility — the understanding to know what I have and don't have. This became very important in my life to go on being successful in my studies and career in years to come.

Speaking about studies, I could not grasp that concept of studying. I was a very poor student academically. I did not do well in my PSLE (137). As a result, I went into the normal technical class. During that period, I was in the Boy's Home and I could not focus as I was going through abuse at the home and my mother was receiving treatment in the hospital.

Upon receiving my results, I remember being told that there was no hope as it was the end of the road for me. It truly seemed like it was the end of the road for me. However, hope came at the right moment. After my PSLE, I left the Boy's Home, and my mum's friend decided to give me a break by taking me to the US for a holiday. Being there gave me a new look at life. It was my first time seeing what I could be and I desired a positive change in my life.

At the start of my secondary school education, I was doing poorly, getting U grades (Ungraded). I was determined to improve. I approached Madam Kahlijah, my Secondary One form teacher, for help. She would stay with me almost every day after school practicing Math questions. She was patient and understanding. I felt heard and needed. What helped the most was that she did not turn me down, but appreciated my efforts. Within 6 months, I scored distinctions in my exams.

What helped was the faith in me to succeed. Without her relentless effort to walk by my side and educate me, I would not have been able to do well, which later on helped me go up to a higher banded academic class a year later.

Perhaps one of the most impactful moments for me was encountering my father for the first time in my life after 15 years. Having grown up without a father, I struggled a lot with my identity. A lot of who I am came from my biological father. Even today, I still do struggle with accepting certain things about myself.

So, when the day came for me to see him for the first time, I knew I was scared of the hurt that I will be experiencing. However, Ms. Sue, together with my mother, accompanied me to the family court for my first encounter with my father after 15 years.

We often take presence for granted. Presence is a powerful gift we can give someone. It provides a safe space for someone to be themselves, space for someone to be heard, and a space to be noticed. That was what Ms. Sue provided for me. I have never cried in front of any stranger before.

However, with the immense pain I felt when I saw my dad, I could not help but cry. Ms. Sue, together with my mother, gave me that safe space to cry. This was an important moment for me, as this experience allowed me to be vulnerable and be myself. In my work as a youth worker, I often give a safe space for youth to express themselves. Sometimes, I will just keep quiet when they need to cry or if they need a moment to collect their thoughts.

Even today, I still journey with two people in my life — Mr. Nick and Mr. Edwyn. Though I am no longer a youth, I am faced with new challenges as an adult. While Mr. Nick journeys with me in my path as a youth worker helps me with life skills, Mr. Edwyn journeys with me with matters close to the heart such as family, relationships, discipline, and being an authentic human being.

In the past, I found it hard to connect with other men and disliked the fact of being under their authority. It was hard for me to allow a man, more so a father figure, into my life as I was taking care of myself. Mr. Edwyn's role in my life in some ways plays that father figure that I needed to hear — the constant challenge to face the truth, which can be scary.

He was there in my darkest moment, continuously telling me to get out of the stinking thinking and move forward. When my mum passed away, Mr. Edwyn and his wife opened their home for me to continue to experience the love of a family which I did not have.

Throughout the years, these special people along with others played a vital role in my growth as a person and as a youth worker. They did what I could not do for myself, which was see the potential I had within me.

When I lost my voice, they became the voices of my battlefield to guide the way. I am thankful for them and to show them gratitude, I decided to pass on what I have received to others through my work — by meeting people where they are and giving them space to work with me.

Supplementary Resources For You — Discount code: NGLPLAYBOOK

All the organisations or entities mentioned here are either startups by Nicholas or those that he assisted with being set up. He continues to use and promote them for his young clients and their respective families:

Personal Website: www.nicholasgabriellim.com

Personal Website: www.nicholasgabriellim.com

1. Clash of the Mind and Heart: Understanding Adolescents (eBook)
2. YouthHack Mobile Training Videos Series by Youth Work Veterans and Experts
   - A Developmental Journey by Dr John Tan (1Hr)
   - Preparing and Transforming Youths by Dr Roland Yeow (1Hr)

- Understanding Gamers and Esports by Nicholas Aaron Khoo (1Hr)
- Vulnerability Is Love by Diane Choo (1Hr)
- Coaching Youths by Joe Chan (1Hr)
- Taking Strained Relationships To Strengths by Tony Leong (1Hr)

3. Podcasts and Videos

Organisation Website: www.nigel.com.sg

Organisation Website: www.nigel.com.sg

1. Attention-deficit hyperactivity disorder (ADHD) non-medicinal treatment and intervention
2. Non-invasive Brain-Computer-Interface (BCI) based Cognitive Development Training – Attention, Memory, Spatial Orientation Skills, Decision Making and Cognitive Flexibility
3. Psychological assessments
    - Youth Level of Service/Case Management Inventory 2.0
    - The Youth Assessment and Screening Instrument
    - The Massachusetts Youth Screening Instrument Version 2

4. Conduct Disorder and Behavioural Intervention
5. Parent and Youth Coaching
6. Life Coaching for Young Professionals
7. Clinical Supervision for Psychologist and Youth Workers

For query, write to: admin@nigel.com.sg

My Working Title Website: https://www.myworkingtitle.xyz/

1. Career SUPERDRIVE™ Board Game (Student Edition)
2. Career SUPERDRIVE™ Student Edition Card Pack
3. 1-on-1 Career Design Coaching (3 online sessions)
4. Career ROADTRIP™ Journal Booklets (Student Edition)
5. Career ROADTRIP™ Digital Journal Booklets (Student Edition)

For query, write to: hello@myworkingtitle.xyz

My Working Title Website: https://www.myworkingtitle.xyz/

Comeback World Website: https://www.comeback.world/

Comeback World Website: https://www.comeback.world/

1. Game Dependency Test
2. Gamer Player Types Test
3. Game Dependency Group Intervention Program
4. Understanding Games Video – https://fb.watch/aWqsbvGXGZ/
5. Understanding Gamers Video – https://fb.watch/aWqorciCCv/

For query, write to: hi@comeback.world

www.ingramcontent.com/pod-product-compliance
Lightning Source LLC
Chambersburg PA
CBHW070308230426
43664CB00015B/2671